Langenscheidt

# German

## at your Fingertips

Tien Tammada

Langenscheidt

# Foreword

Traveling to foreign or distant lands is a wonderful and exciting thing to do. In fact it probably features top of the list in worldwide rankings.

However, before every journey to a foreign country, there is a hurdle to be cleared, and this hurdle is called "foreign languages". For many, this hurdle seems insurmountable. As a result, they have to give up their life's dream.

What a pity!

You may be planning a week's holiday in Germany to experience the magical countryside or considering moving to live and work in a German-speaking country.

Whatever your motivation, don't wait.
Don't let this hurdle stop you from fulfilling your lifelong dream!
Have the courage to embark on this exciting journey to the German language – **now!**

Once you've made the decision, you'll find that this book provides you with the first helpful steps. You don't need to book a language course and you don't need to worry about complicated grammatical points.

Anyone who has learnt to master a foreign language knows that the essential and really crucial thing about learning a language is actually quite simple: you need to jump in at the deep end. Once you're in the water, everything flows from there.

Jump and don't think twice! You'll learn by doing, not by preparing. The pictures, the selection of important words and useful phrases that you'll find in this book are an important first step. As soon as you come up against the first language hurdle, you can open the book at the appropriate page and find the necessary words and phrases.

If that doesn't work, try pointing to the relevant picture or sentence with your finger. People will know immediately what you mean.
It's really all very easy and convenient. That's why the book is called **"German at your Fingertips"**.

# Content

# Useful daily conversations

Alltagssätze, Alltagsschätze
[ˈalˌtaːks ˈzɛt͡sə ˈalˌtaːks ˈʃɛt͡sə]

## Greeting

Begrüßung
[bəˈɡʁyːsʊŋ]

| | | | |
|---|---|---|---|
| Hallo! | Guten Morgen! | Guten Tag! | Guten Abend! |
| [haˈloː] | [ˌguː.tən̩ ˈmɔʁgn̩] | [ˌguː.tən ˈtaːk] | [ˌguː.tən ˈaː.bənt] |
| Hello! | Good morning! | Good afternoon! | Good evening! |

**Wie geht es Ihnen?/ Wie geht es dir?**

[viː geːt ɛs ˈiːnən / viː geːt ɛs diːɐ̯]

How are you?

**Es geht mir gut, danke.**

[ɛs geːt miːɐ̯ guːt ˈdaŋkə]

I'm fine, thank you.

| Ja. | Nein. |
| --- | --- |
| [jaː] | [naɪ̯n] |
| Yes. | No. |

| Danke. | Vielen Dank. | Gern geschehen. | Mit Vergnügen. |
| --- | --- | --- | --- |
| [ˈdaŋkə] | [ˈfiːlən ˈdaŋk] | [gɛʁn gəˈʃeːən] | [mɪt fɛɐ̯ˈgnyːgn̩] |
| Thanks. | Thank you very much. | You're welcome. | With pleasure. |

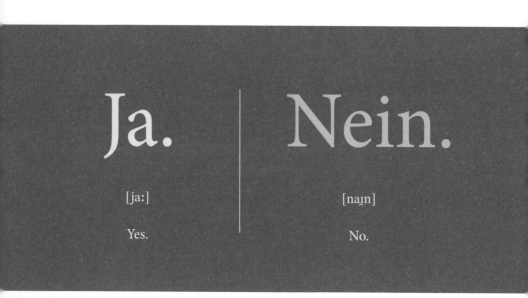

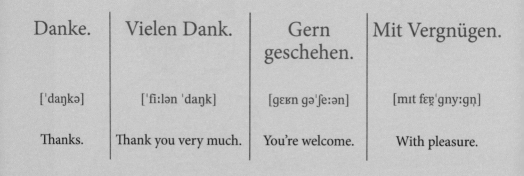

| | |
|---|---|
| Ich heiße... [ɪç ˈhaɪ̯sə] | My name is… |
| Wie heißen Sie/ heißt du? [viː ˈhaɪ̯sn̩ ziː haɪ̯st duː] | What is your name? |
| Sehr erfreut. [zeːɐ̯ ɛɐ̯ˈfʁɔɪ̯t] | Nice to meet you. |
| Ich komme aus den vereinigten Staaten von Amerika. [ɪç ˈkɔmə aʊ̯s deːn fɛɐ̯ˈʔaɪ̯nɪçtən ˈʃtaːtn̩ fɔn aˈmeːʁɪka] | I'm from the United States of America. |
| Ich spreche kein Deutsch. [ɪç ˈʃpʁɛçə kaɪ̯n dɔɪ̯tʃ] | I cannot speak German. |
| Ich spreche ein bisschen Deutsch. [ɪç ˈʃpʁɛçə aɪ̯n ˈbɪsçən dɔɪ̯tʃ] | I can speak a little German. |
| Wie heißt das auf Deutsch? [vi: haɪ̯st das aʊ̯f dɔɪ̯tʃ] | How do you say that in German? |
| Könnten Sie/ Könntest du das bitte wiederholen? [ˈkœntn̩ ziː ˈkœntəst duː das ˈbɪtə ˌviːdɐˈhoːlən] | Could you repeat that, please? |
| Könnten Sie/ Könntest du bitte etwas langsamer sprechen? [ˈkœntn̩ ziː ˈkœntəst duː ˈbɪtə ˈɛtvas ˈlaŋˌzaːmɐ ˈʃpʁɛçn̩] | Could you speak a little more slowly, please? |

| | |
|---|---|
| Was bedeutet das?<br>[vas bəˈdɔ̯ɪtət̩ das] | What does that mean? |
| Was ist das?<br>[vas ɪst das] | What is that? |
| Wie bitte?<br>[viː ˈbɪtə] | Pardon? |
| Entschuldigung.<br>[ɛntˈʃʊldɪgʊŋ] | Excuse me. |
| Kein Problem.<br>[ka̯ɪn pʁoˈbleːm] | No problem. |
| Wo bin ich?<br>[voː bɪn ɪç] | Where am I? |
| Wie komme ich zum...?<br>[viː ˈkɔmə ɪç tsʊm] | How do I get to...? |
| Herr<br>[hɛʁ] | Mister |

| | |
|---|---|
| Frau (verheiratete Frau)<br>[fʁaʊ̯ (fɛɐ̯ˈhaɪ̯ʁaːtətə fʁaʊ)] | Mrs. |
| Frau (unverheiratete Frau)<br>[fʁaʊ (ˈʊnfɛɐ̯haɪ̯ʁaːtətə̯ fʁaʊ)] | Ms. |
| Wo ist...?<br>[voː ɪst] | Where is...? |
| Ich hätte gern...<br>[ɪç ˈhɛtə gɛʁn] | I would like... |
| Wie viel kostet das?<br>[viː fiːl koːstət das] | How much does it cost? |
| Ich mag das.<br>[ɪç maːk das] | I like this. |
| Ich mag das nicht.<br>[ɪç maːk das nɪçt] | I don't like that. |
| So lala.<br>[ˈzoː ˌlaˌla] | So-so. |

| | |
|---|---|
| Wunderbar!<br>[ˈvʊndɐbaːɐ̯] | Wonderful! |
| Hervorragend!<br>[hɛɐ̯ˈfoːɐ̯ˌʁaːɡn̩t] | Great! |
| Perfekt!<br>[pɛʁˈfɛkt] | Perfect! |
| gut<br>[ɡuːt] | good |
| sehr gut<br>[zeːɐ̯ ɡuːt] | very good |
| schlecht<br>[ʃlɛçt] | bad |
| sehr schlecht<br>[ʃlɛçt] | very bad |
| viel<br>[fiːl] | a lot |
| wenig<br>[ˈveːnɪç] | little, few |
| ein bisschen<br>[aɪ̯n ˈbɪsçən] | some, a bit of |
| Einen Moment, bitte.<br>[ˈaɪ̯nən moˈmɛnt ˈbɪtə] | One moment, please. |
| Einen Augenblick, bitte.<br>[ˈaɪ̯nən aʊ̯ɡn̩ˈblɪk ˈbɪtə] | Just a moment, please. |

| | |
|---|---|
| Bis bald!<br>[bɪs balt] | See you soon! |
| Bis später!<br>[bɪs ˈʃpɛːtɐ] | See you later! |
| Bis morgen!<br>[bɪs ˈmɔʁgn̩] | See you tomorrow! |
| Auf Wiedersehen!<br>[aʊ̯f ˈviːdɐˌzeːən] | Good bye! |
| Tschüss<br>[tʃyːs] | Bye! |
| Wer?<br>[veːɐ̯] | Who? |
| Was?<br>[vas] | What? |
| Wo?<br>[voː] | Where? |
| Wann?<br>[van] | When? |
| Warum?<br>[vaˈrʊm] | Why? |
| Wie?<br>[viː] | How? |
| Wie viel(e)?<br>[viː fiːl(ə)] | How much?/ How many? |

der Flughafen
[de:ɐ̯ 'flu:kha:fn̩]
the airport

Wo ist die Passkontrolle?
[vo: ɪst di: 'paskɔn,tʁɔlə]
Where is passport control?

# Das Flugzeug

[das 'flu:k,t͡sɔɪ̯k]

Entschuldigung, wie komme ich zum Stadtzentrum?
[ɛnt'ʃʊldɪgʊŋ vi: 'kɔmə ɪç tsʊm 'ʃtat,t͡sɛntʁʊm]
Excuse me, how can I get to the city centre?

Wo ist der Bahnhof?
[vo: ɪst de:ɐ̯'ba:n,ho:f]
Where is the train station?

AUSGANG

## Entschuldigung, wo ist der Ausgang?

[ɛntˈʃʊldɪɡʊŋ voː ɪst deːɐ̯ ˈaʊ̯sˌɡaŋ]

Excuse me, where is the exit?

the airplane

Wo ist die Bushaltestelle?

[voː ɪst diː ˈbʊshaltəʃtɛlə]

Where is the bus stop?

Wo bekomme ich ein Taxi?
[voː bəˈkɔmə ɪç aɪ̯n ˈtaksi]
Where can I get a taxi?

Wo ist die Touristeninformation?
[voː ɪst diː tuˈʁɪstn̩ʔɪnfɔʁmaˌt͡si̯oːn]
Where is tourist information?

Wie weit ist es bis zum Stadtzentrum?
[viː vai̯t ɪst ɛs bɪs t͡sʊm ˈʃtatˌt͡sɛntʁʊm]
How far is it to the city centre?

Können Sie mir ein preiswertes Hotel empfehlen?
[ˈkœnən ziː miːɐ̯ ai̯n ˈpʁai̯sˌveːɐ̯təs hoˈtɛl ɛmˈp͡feːlən]
Can you recommend an inexpensive hotel?

Fahren Sie mich bitte zu dieser Adresse.
[ˈfaːʁən ziː mɪç ˈbɪtə t͡sʊm ˈdiːzɐ aˈdʁɛsə]
Drive me to this address, please.

TAXI

das Taxi
[das ˈtaksi]

taxi

Wie viel  kostet die Fahrt?
[viː ˈfiːl ˈkoːstət diː faːɐ̯t]
How much does the ride cost?

Kann ich mit Kreditkarte bezahlen?
[kan ɪç mɪt kʁeˈdɪtˌkaʁtə bəˈʦaːlən]
Can I pay by credit card?

Würden Sie mir bitte sagen, wann ich aussteigen muss?
[ˈvʏʁdən ziː miːɐ̯ ˈbɪtə ˈzaːgn̩ van ɪç aʊ̯sˌʃtaɪ̯gn̩ mʊs]
Could you tell me when to get off please?

Vielen Dank für Ihre/ deine Hilfe.
[ˈfiːlən daŋk fyːɐ̯ ˈiːʁə/ ˈdaɪ̯nə ˈhɪlfə]
Thank you very much for your help.

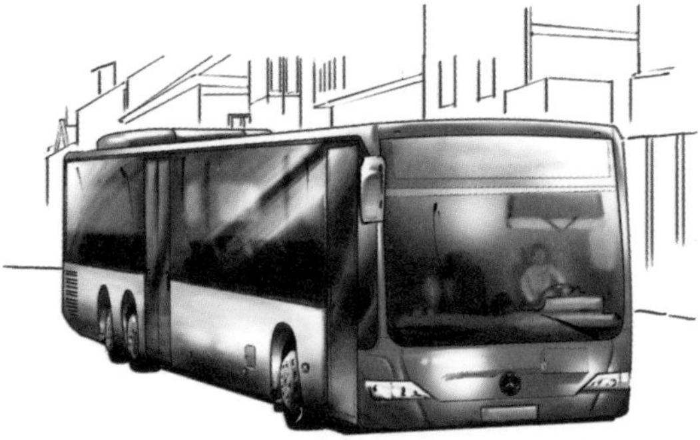

der Bus
[deːɐ̯ bʊs]

bus

der Zug

[deːɐ̯ t͡suːk]

train

5013-G

die U-Bahn

[diː ˈuːˌbaːn]

underground

die Straßenbahn

[diː ˈʃtʁaːsn̩ˌbaːn]

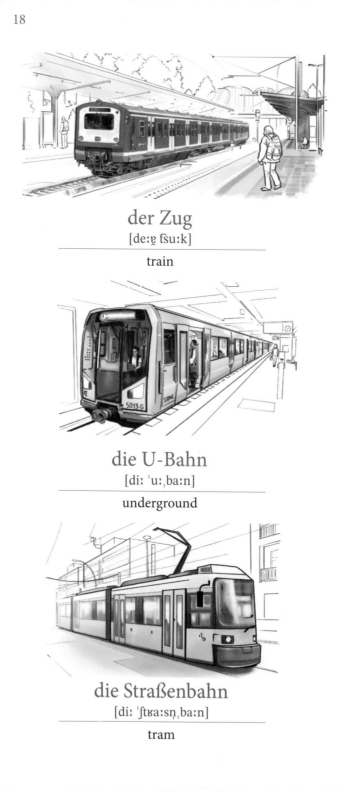

tram

der Hochgeschwindigkeitszug

[deːɐ̯ ˈhoːxɡəʃvɪndɪçkaɪ̯t͡sˌt͡suːk]

HST (High Speed Train)

das Schiff

[das ʃɪf]

ship

# Accommodation

Die Unterkunft [diː ˈʊntɐˌkʊnft]

| | |
|---|---|
| Haben Sie ein Zimmer frei?<br>[ˈhaːbən ziː aɪ̯n ˈt͡sɪmɐ fʁaɪ̯] | Is there any room available? |
| Könnte ich mir das Zimmer ansehen?<br>[kœntə ɪç miːɐ das ˈt͡sɪmɐ anzeːən] | May I see the room, please? |
| Wie viel kostet das?<br>[viː fiːl ˈkoːstət das] | How much is it? |
| Ist das Frühstück inbegriffen?<br>[ɪst das ˈfʁyːʃtʏk ɪnbəˌɡʁɪfn̩] | Is breakfast included? |
| Ich habe ein Zimmer<br>auf den Namen... gebucht.<br>[ɪç ˈhaːbə aɪ̯n ˈt͡sɪmɐ aʊ̯f deːn<br>ˈnaːmən ɡəˈbuːxt] | I have booked a room<br>in the name of... |

Hier ist mein Reisepass.
[hiːɐ̯ ɪst ˈmaɪ̯n ˈʁaɪ̯zəˌpas]
Here is my passport.

Gibt es hier WLAN?
[giːpt ɛs hiːɐ ˈveːlaːn]
Do you have wireless Internet?

Gibt es einen Safe?
[giːpt ɛs ˈaɪ̯nən seːf]
Do you have a safe?

Wann muss ich auschecken?
[van mʊs ɪç aʊ̯s ˈʃɛkn̩]
When do I have to check out?

Ist die Rezeption Tag und Nacht geöffnet?
[ɪst diː ˌʁet͡sɛpˈt͡si̯oːn taːk ʊnt̥ naxt gəˈʔœfnət]
Is reception open all the time?

# Ich hätte gern ein Zimmer für...

[ɪç ˈhɛtə gɛʁn aɪ̯n ˈt͡sɪmɐ fyːɐ̯]

I would like a room for…

eine Person
[ˈaɪ̯nə pɛʁˈzoːn]
one (person).

zwei Personen
[t͡svaɪ̯ pɛʁˈzoːnən]
two (persons).

eine Familie
[ˈaɪ̯nə faˈmiːli̯ə]
a family.

die Decke
[diː ˈdɛkə]
ceiling
das Bücherregal
[das byːçɐʁeˌgaːl]
bookshelf
die Lampe
[diː ˈlampə]
lamp
das Fenster
[das ˈfɛnstɐ]
window
der Lichtschalter
[deːɐ̯ ˈlɪçtˌʃaltɐ]
light switch
der Wecker
[deːɐ̯ ˈvɛkɐ]
alarm clock
das Kopfkissen
[das kɔp͡fˌkɪsn̩]
pillow
der Stuhl
[deːɐ̯ ʃtuːl]
chair
der Schreibtisch
[deːɐ̯ ˈʃʁaɪ̯pˌtɪʃ]
desk
die Steckdose
[diː ˈʃtɛkdoːzə]
electric socket

die Klimaanlage
[diː ˈkliːmaˌʔanlaːgə]
air conditioner
der Vorhang
[deːɐ̯ ˈfoːɐ̯haŋ]
curtain
der Kleiderbügel
[deːɐ̯ ˈklaɪ̯dɐˌbyːgl̩]
clothes hanger
der Hut
[deːɐ̯ huːt]
hat
die Schublade
[diː ˈʃuːplaːdə]
drawer
die Handtasche
[diː ˈhanttaʃə]
handbag
die T-shirts
[diː ˈtiːˌʃøːɐ̯t͡s]
T-shirts
die Hosen
[diː ˈhoːzə]
trousers
die Schuhe
[diː ˈʃuːə]
shoes
der Teppich
[deːɐ̯ ˈtɛpɪç]
carpet
die Decke
[diː ˈdɛkə]
blanket
das Bett
[das bɛt]
bed

# In the bedroom

Im Schlafzimmer [ɪm ˈʃlaːfˌt͡sɪmɐ]

# In the bathroom

Im Badezimmer [ɪm ˈbaːdəˌt͡sɪmɐ]

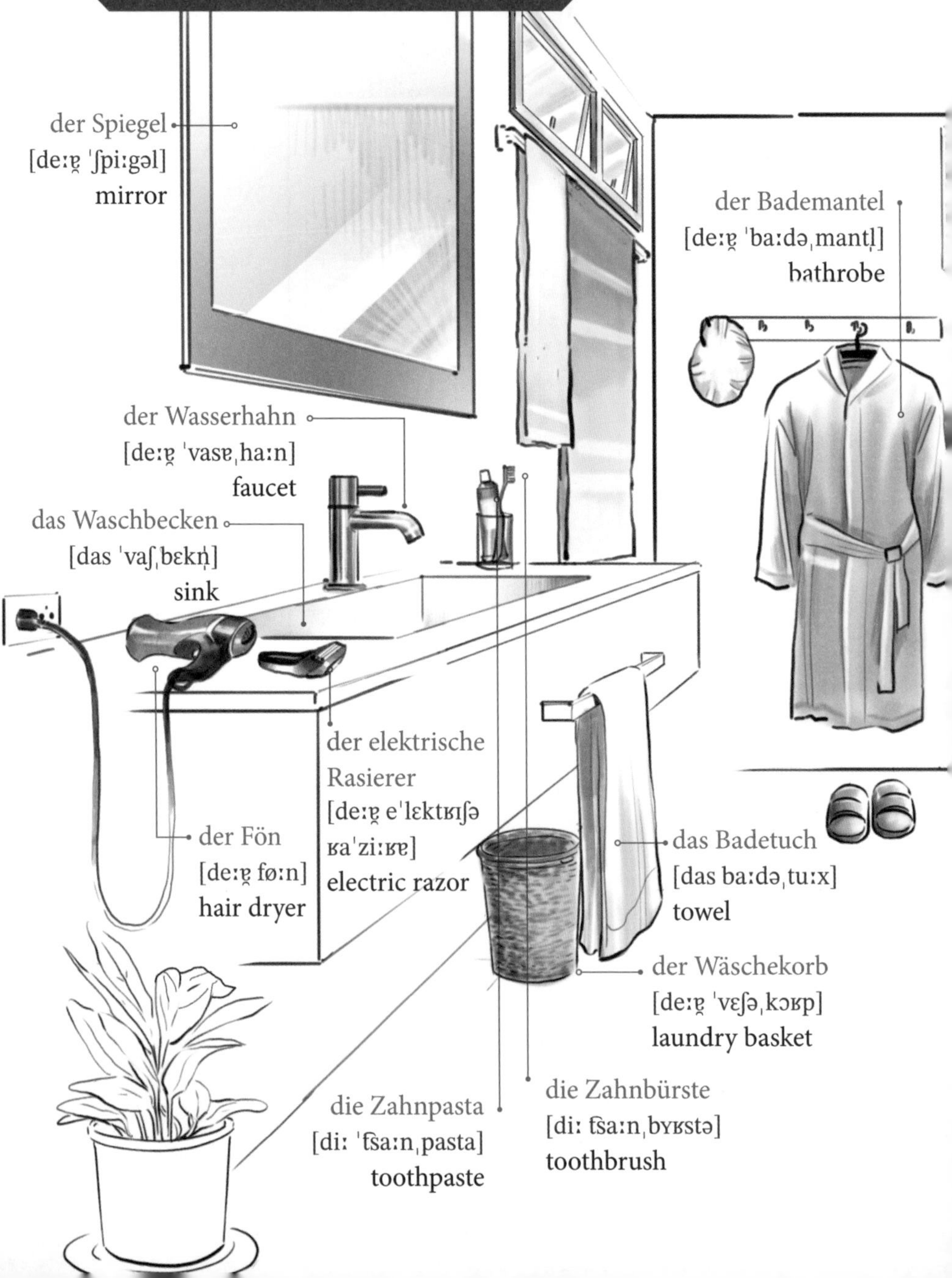
der Spiegel
[deːɐ̯ ˈʃpiːgəl]
mirror
der Bademantel
[deːɐ̯ ˈbaːdəˌmantl̩]
bathrobe
der Wasserhahn
[deːɐ̯ ˈvasɐˌhaːn]
faucet
das Waschbecken
[das ˈvaʃˌbɛkn̩]
sink
der elektrische Rasierer
[deːɐ̯ eˈlɛktʁɪʃə ʁaˈziːʁɐ]
electric razor
der Fön
[deːɐ̯ føːn]
hair dryer
das Badetuch
[das baːdəˌtuːx]
towel
der Wäschekorb
[deːɐ̯ ˈvɛʃəˌkɔʁp]
laundry basket
die Zahnpasta
[diː ˈt͡saːnˌpasta]
toothpaste
die Zahnbürste
[diː t͡saːnˌbʏʁstə]
toothbrush

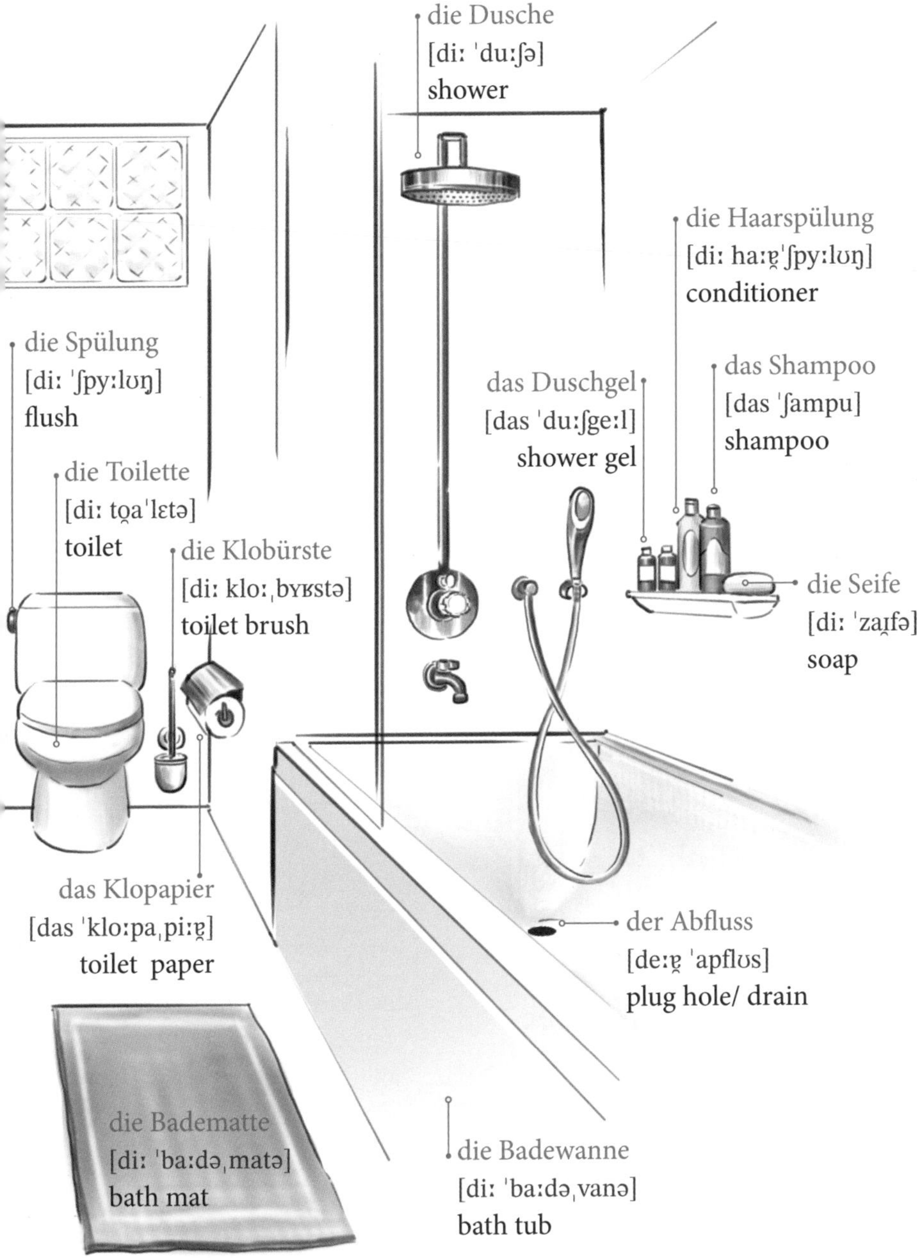
die Dusche
[diː ˈduːʃə]
shower
die Haarspülung
[diː haːɐ̯ˈʃpyːlʊŋ]
conditioner
die Spülung
[diː ˈʃpyːlʊŋ]
flush
das Duschgel
[das ˈduːʃgeːl]
shower gel
das Shampoo
[das ˈʃampu]
shampoo
die Toilette
[diː to̯aˈlɛtə]
toilet
die Klobürste
[diː kloːˌbʏʁstə]
toilet brush
die Seife
[diː ˈzaɪ̯fə]
soap
das Klopapier
[das ˈkloːpaˌpiːɐ̯]
toilet paper
der Abfluss
[deːɐ̯ ˈapflʊs]
plug hole/ drain
die Badematte
[diː ˈbaːdəˌmatə]
bath mat
die Badewanne
[diː ˈbaːdəˌvanə]
bath tub

der Schrank
[deːɐ̯ ʃʁaŋk]
cabinet
die Uhr
[diː uːɐ̯]
clock
der Fernsehapparat
[deːɐ̯ ˈfɛʁnzeːʔapa ˌʁaːt]
television
der Kaffeeautomat
[deːɐ̯ ˈkafeʔaʊ̯toˌmaːt]
coffee machine
die Stereoanlage
[diːˈʃteʁeoˌʔanlaːɡə]
stereo
der Lautsprecher
[deːɐ̯ ˈlaʊ̯tˌʃpʁɛçɐ]
loud speaker
der Barhocker
[deːɐ̯ ˈbaːɐ̯ˌhɔkɐ]
bar stool
der Ventilator
[deːɐ̯ vɛntiˈlaːtoːɐ̯]
fan

# In the living room

Im Wohnzimmer [ɪm ˈvoːnˌt͡sɪmɐ]

die Lampe
[diː ˈlampə]
lamp
das Klavier
[das klaˈviːɐ̯]
piano
das Bild
[das bɪlt]
picture
die Bücher
[diː ˈbyːçɐ]
books
der Sessel
[deːɐ̯ ˈzɛsl̩]
armchair
die Geige
[diː ˈɡaɪ̯ɡə]
violin
der Tisch
[deːɐ̯ tɪʃ]
table
das Telefon
[das ˈteːləfoːn]
telephone
das Sofa
[das ˈzoːfa]
sofa
die Vase
[diː ˈvaːzə]
vase
die Fernbedienung
[diː ˈfɛʁnbəˌdiːnʊŋ]
remote control
die Blumen
[diː ˈbluːmən]
flowers

die Pfanne
[diː ˈp͡fanə]
frying pan
die Tasse
[diː ˈtasə]
cup
die Flasche
[diː ˈflaʃə]
bottle
das Weinglas
[das ˈva͡ɪnˌɡlaːs]
wine glass
der Teller
[deːɐ̯ ˈtɛlɐ]
plate
der Schneebesen
[deːɐ̯ ˈʃneːbeːzn̩]
whisk
der Löffel
[deːɐ̯ ˈlœfəl]
spoon
die Gabel
[diː ˈɡaːbəl]
fork
das Schneidebrett
[das ˈʃna͡ɪdəˌbʁɛt]
chopping board
der Wasserhahn
[deːɐ̯ ˈvasɐˌhaːn]
faucet
die Mikrowelle
[diː ˈmiːkʁoˌvɛlə]
microwave

# In the kitchen

In der Küche [ɪn deːɐ̯ ˈkʏçə]

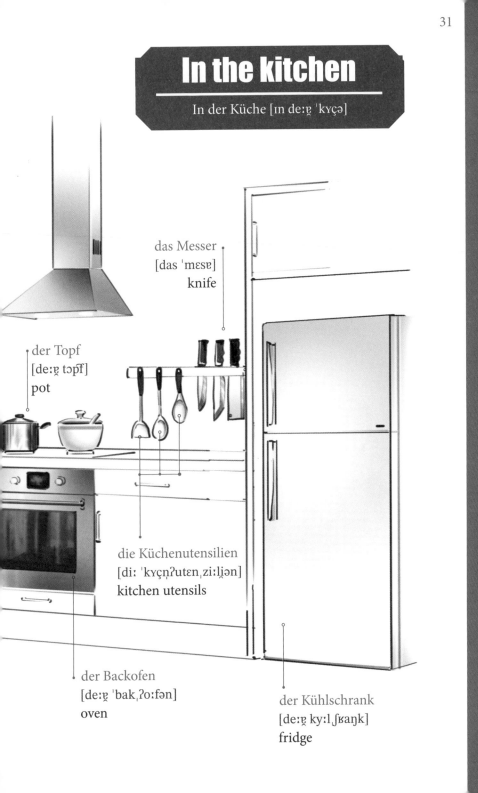

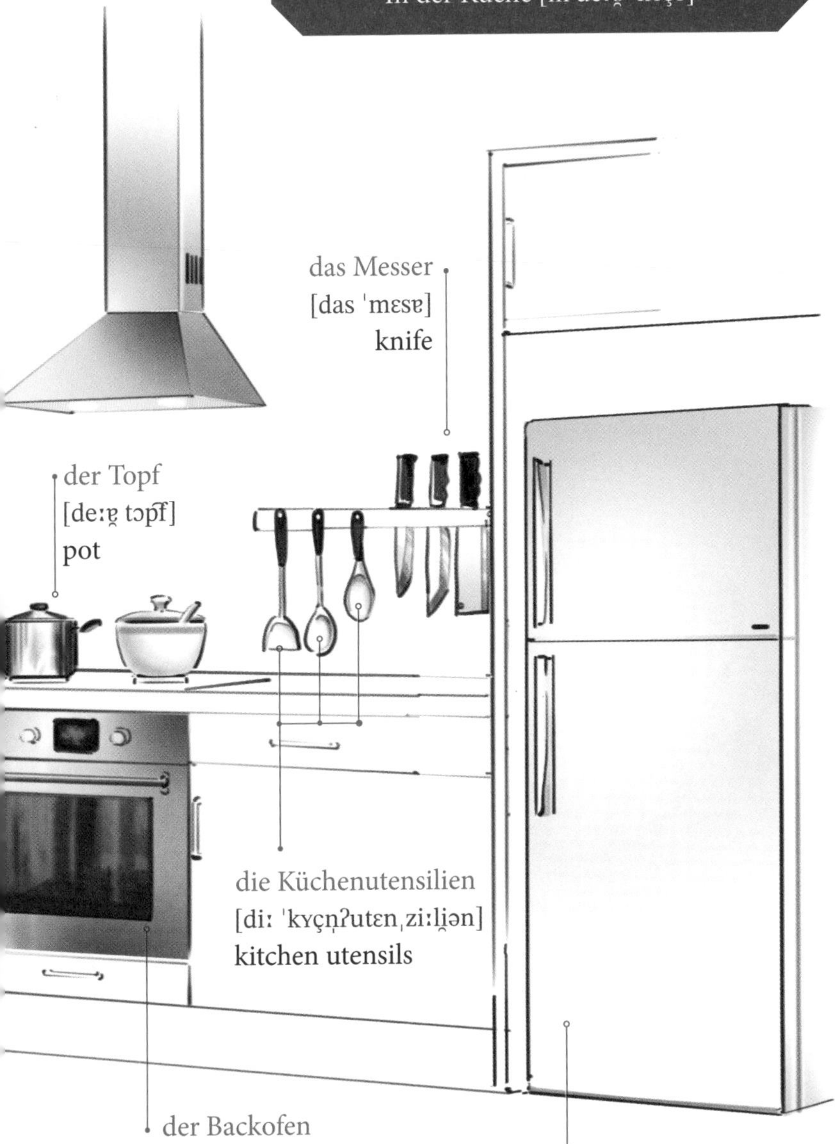
das Messer
[das ˈmɛsɐ]
knife
der Topf
[deːɐ̯ tɔp͡f]
pot
die Küchenutensilien
[diː ˈkʏçn̩ʔutɛnˌziːli̯ən]
kitchen utensils
der Backofen
[deːɐ̯ ˈbakˌʔoːfən]
oven
der Kühlschrank
[deːɐ̯ kyːlˌʃʁaŋk]
fridge

# Excursions (in the city and in the countryside)

Ausflüge (in der Stadt und außerhalb)
['aʊ̯sˌflyːgə ɪn deːɐ̯ ʃtat ʊnt 'aʊ̯sɐhalp]

**Welche Sehenswürdigkeiten gibt es hier?**

[vɛlçə 'zeːənsvʏʁdɪçˌkaɪ̯tn̩ giːpt ɛs hiːɐ̯]

Are there any tourist attractions in this area?

## Wo kann ich regionale Spezialitäten probieren?

[voː kan ɪç ʁegi̯oˈnaːlə ʃpet͡si̯aliˈtɛːtn̩ pʁoˈbiːʁən]

Where can I taste the traditional local food?

ABHIJA

# Excursions by train

Ausflüge mit dem Zug [ˈaʊ̯sˌflyːɡə mɪt deːm t͡suːk]

| | |
|---|---|
| Wo ist der Bahnhof?<br>[voː ɪst deːɐ̯ˈbaːnˌhoːf] | Where is the train station? |
| Wo ist der Fahrkartenautomat?<br>[voː ɪst deːɐ̯ ˈfaːɐ̯kaʁtn̩ʔaʊ̯toˌmaːt] | Where is the ticket vending machine? |
| Wo ist der Fahrkartenschalter?<br>[voː ɪst deːɐ̯ ˈfaːɐ̯kaʁtn̩ˌʃaltɐ] | Where is the ticket office? |
| Wie viel kostet die Fahrkarte?<br>[viː fiːl ˈkoːstət diː ˈfaːɐ̯ˌkaʁtə] | How much does the ticket cost? |
| Bitte eine Fahrkarte erster Klasse.<br>[ˈbɪtə ˈaɪ̯nə ˈfaːɐ̯ˌkaʁtə ˈeːɐ̯stə ˈklasə] | One first-class ticket, please. |
| Bitte eine Fahrkarte zweiter Klasse.<br>[ˈbɪtə ˈaɪ̯nə ˈfaːɐ̯ˌkaʁtə ˈt͡svaɪ̯tɐ ˈklasə] | One second-class ticket, please. |
| Bitte eine einfache Fahrkarte.<br>[ˈbɪtə ˈaɪ̯nə ˈaɪ̯nfaxə ˈfaːɐ̯ˌkaʁtə] | A one-way ticket, please. |

| | |
|---|---|
| Bitte eine Rückfahrkarte.<br>[ˈbɪtə ˈaɪ̯nə ˈʁʏkfaːɐ̯ˌkaʁtə] | A return ticket, please. |
| Ich möchte einen Sitzplatz reservieren.<br>[ɪç ˈmœçtə ˈaɪ̯nən ˈzɪt͡sˌplat͡s ʁezɛʁˈviːʁən] | I would like to reserve a seat please. |
| Wann fährt der Zug ab?<br>[van fɛːɐ̯t deːɐ̯ t͡suːk ap] | What time does the train leave? |
| Wie oft muss ich umsteigen?<br>[viː ɔft mʊs ɪç ˈʊmˌʃtaɪ̯ɡn̩] | How many times do I have to change trains? |
| Wie heißt die nächste Haltestelle?<br>[viː haɪ̯st diː ˈnɛːçstə ˈhaltəʃtɛlə] | What is the next station called? |
| Würden Sie mir bitte sagen, wann ich aussteigen muss?<br>[ˈvʏʁdən ziː miːɐ̯ ˈbɪtə ˈzaːɡn̩ van ɪç ˈaʊ̯sˌʃtaɪ̯ɡn̩ mʊs] | Please tell me when I have to get off. |

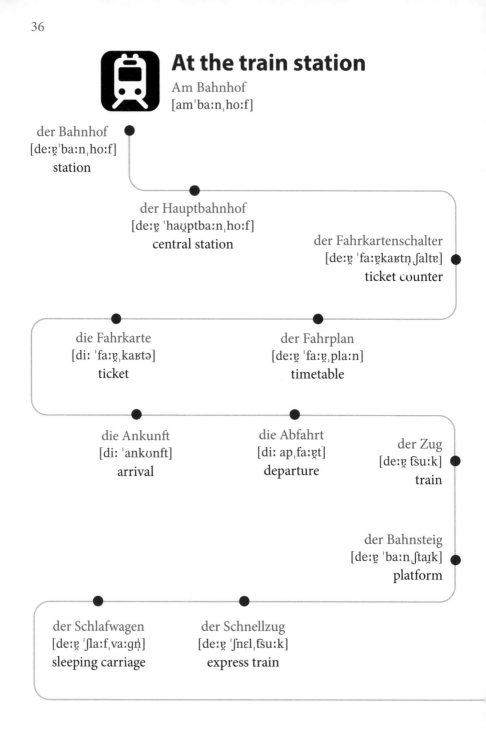

# At the train station

Am Bahnhof
[amˈbaːnˌhoːf]

der Bahnhof
[deːɐ̯ˈbaːnˌhoːf]
station

der Hauptbahnhof
[deːɐ̯ ˈhau̯ptbaːnˌhoːf]
central station

der Fahrkartenschalter
[deːɐ̯ ˈfaːɐ̯kaʁtn̩ˌʃaltɐ]
ticket counter

die Fahrkarte
[diː ˈfaːɐ̯ˌkaʁtə]
ticket

der Fahrplan
[deːɐ̯ ˈfaːɐ̯ˌplaːn]
timetable

die Ankunft
[diː ˈankʊnft]
arrival

die Abfahrt
[diː apˌfaːɐ̯t]
departure

der Zug
[deːɐ̯ t͡suːk]
train

der Bahnsteig
[deːɐ̯ ˈbaːnˌʃtai̯k]
platform

der Schlafwagen
[deːɐ̯ ˈʃlaːfˌvaːgn̩]
sleeping carriage

der Schnellzug
[deːɐ̯ ˈʃnɛlˌt͡suːk]
express train

eine Fahrkarte erster Klasse
[ˈai̯nə ˈfaːɐ̯ˌkaʁtə ˈeːɐ̯stɐˈklasə]
first-class ticket

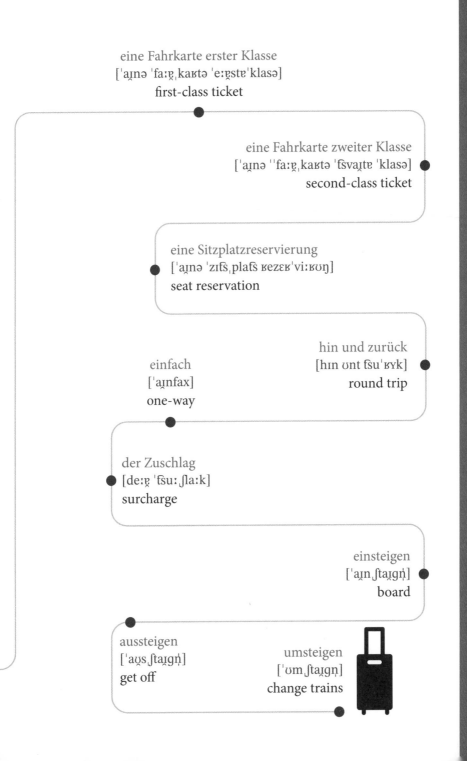

eine Fahrkarte zweiter Klasse
[ˈai̯nə ˈˈfaːɐ̯ˌkaʁtə ˈt͡svai̯tɐ ˈklasə]
second-class ticket

eine Sitzplatzreservierung
[ˈai̯nə ˈzɪt͡sˌplat͡s ʁezɛʁˈviːʁʊŋ]
seat reservation

hin und zurück
[hɪn ʊnt t͡suˈʁʏk]
round trip

einfach
[ˈai̯nfax]
one-way

der Zuschlag
[deːɐ̯ ˈt͡suːˌʃlaːk]
surcharge

einsteigen
[ˈai̯nˌʃtai̯gn̩]
board

aussteigen
[ˈau̯sˌʃtai̯gn̩]
get off

umsteigen
[ˈʊmˌʃtai̯gn̩]
change trains

## Um wie viel Uhr fährt der Zug / der Bus / die U-Bahn / die Straßenbahn ab?

[ʊm viː fiːl uːɐ̯ fɛːɐ̯t deːɐ̯ t͡suːk /
deːɐ̯ bʊs / diː ˈuːbaːn / diː ˈʃtʁaːsn̩ˌbaːn ap]

What time does the train / the bus /
the underground / the tram leave?

**Entschuldigen Sie bitte,
könnten Sie mir helfen,
ein Ticket an dem Automaten zu kaufen?**

[ɛntˈʃʊldɪgn̩ ziː ˈbɪtə
kœntn̩ ziː miːɐ̯ ˈhɛlfn̩
aɪ̯n ˈtɪkət an deːm aʊ̯toˈmaːtn̩ t͡suː ˈkaʊ̯fn̩]

Excuse me, can you help me to buy
a ticket from the machine please?

Fahrkarten
16

**Ich möchte nach ... fahren.**

[ɪç ˈmœçtə naːx ˈfaːʁən]

I want to go to …

# Excursions by bus and tram

Ausflüge mit dem Bus und mit der Straßenbahn

[ˈaʊ̯sˌfly:gə mɪt de:m bʊs ʊnt mɪt de:ɐ̯ ˈʃtʁa:sn̩ˌba:n]

| | |
|---|---|
| der Bus<br>[de:ɐ̯ bʊs] | bus |
| die Bushaltestelle<br>[di: ˈbʊshaltəʃtɛlə] | bus stop |
| die Straßenbahn<br>[di: ˈʃtʁa:sn̩ˌba:n] | tram |

**Wo ist die Straßenbahnhaltestelle?**

[vo: ɪst di: ˈʃtʁa:sn̩ˌba:nˌhaltəʃtɛlə]

Where is the tram stop?

| | |
|---|---|
| die Straßenbahnhaltestelle<br>[di: ˈʃtra:sn̩ba:nˌhaltəʃtɛlə] | tram stop |
| die Fahrkarte<br>[di: ˈfa:ɐ̯ˌkaʁtə] | ticket |
| der Kontrolleur<br>[de:ɐ̯ kɔnˈtʁɔlɐ] | ticket inspector |
| die Geldstrafe<br>[di: ˈgɛltˌʃtʁa:fə] | fine / penalty |

# Wo ist ...?

[voː ɪst]

Where is…?

## Wo ist die Bushaltestelle?

[voː ɪst diː ˈbʊshaltəʃtɛlə]

Where is the bus stop?

## die Ampel

[diː ˈampl̩]

traffic light

## das Motorrad

[das ˈmoːtoːɐ̯ˌʁaːt]

motorcycle

## das Fahrrad

[das ˈfaːɐ̯ˌʁaːt]

bicycle

## das Auto

[das ˈaʊ̯to]

car

# Travelling on your own by car, motocycle, bicycle and on foot

Auf eigene Faust unterwegs mit dem Auto, Motorrad, Fahrrad und zu Fuß.
[au̯f ˈaɪ̯gənə fau̯st ʊntɐˈveːks mɪt deːm ˈau̯toː moːtoːɐ̯ˌʁaːt ˈfaːɐ̯ˌʁaːt ʊnt t͡suː fuːs]

| | |
|---|---|
| die Straße<br>[diː ˈʃtʁaːsə] | street |
| die Kreuzung<br>[diː ˈkʁɔɪ̯t͡sʊŋ] | intersection |
| geradeaus gehen/fahren<br>[gəʁaːdəˈʔau̯s ˈgeːən/ˈfaːʁən] | go straight on |
| rechts abbiegen<br>[ʁɛçt͡s ˈapˌbiːgn̩] | turn right |
| links abbiegen<br>[lɪŋks ˈapˌbiːgn̩] | turn left |
| Wo ist eine Tankstelle?<br>[voː ɪst ˈaɪ̯nə ˈtaŋkʃtɛlə] | Where is a petrol station? |
| hier<br>[hiːɐ̯] | here |
| dort<br>[dɔʁt] | over there |
| nah<br>[naː] | near |
| weit<br>[vaɪ̯t] | far |
| Welches Benzin soll ich tanken?<br>[vɛlçəs bɛnˈt͡siːn zɔl ɪç ˈtaŋkn̩] | What kind of petrol should I put in? |

# Art and leisure time activities

Kunst und Freizeitaktivitäten [kʊnst ʊnt ˈfʁaɪ̯ˌt͡saɪ̯taktiviˈtɛːtn̩]

das Theater
[das teˈaːtɐ]
the theatre

THEATRE

das Opernhaus
[das ˈoːpɐnˌhaʊ̯s]
the opera house

das Kino
[das ˈkiːno]
the cinema

die Kunstgalerie
[diː ˈkʊnstgaləˌʁiː]
the art gallery

das Museum
[das muˈzeːʊm]
the museum

M

das Hallenbad
[das ˈhalənˌbaːt]
the indoor swimming pool

das Freibad
[das ˈfʁaɪ̯ˌbaːt]
the outdoor swimming pool

die Sauna
[diː ˈzaʊ̯na]
the sauna

der Stadtpark
[deːɐ̯ ˈʃtatˌpaʁk]
the city park

das Fitnessstudio
[das ˈfɪtnɛsˌʃtuːdi̯o]
the fitness centre

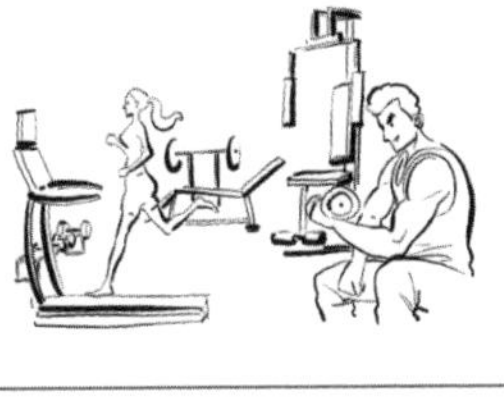

# Tourist attractions

Sehenswürdigkeiten [ˈzeːənsvʏʁdɪçˌkaɪ̯tn̩]

Rhein
[raɪ̯n]

Frauenkirche (Dresden)
[ˈfʁaʊ̯ənˌkɪʁçə]

Schwarzwald
[ˈʃvaʁt͡svalt]

Brandenburger Tor (Berlin)
[bʁandn̩ˌbʊʁgɐ toːɐ̯]

Kölner Dom (Köln)
[kœlnɐ doːm]

Miniatur Wunderland (Hamburg)
[mini̯aˈtuːɐ̯ ˈvʊndɐlɑnt]

Heidelberg
[hai̯dl̩bɛʁk]

# Tourist attractions

Sehenswürdigkeiten [ˈzeːənsvʏʁdɪçˌkaɪ̯tn]

Rügen
[ʁyːgn̩]

Rothenburg ob der Tauber
(Bayern)
[ˈʁoːtn̩ˌbʊʁk ɔp deːɐ̯ ˈtaʊ̯bɐ]

Museumsinsel (Berlin)
[muˈzeːʊmsˈɪnzl̩]

Altstadt von Hamburg
[ˈaltʃtat fɔn ˈhambʊʁk]

Schloss Neuschwanstein (Füssen)
[ʃlɔs nɔɪ̯ʃvaːn ʃtaɪ̯n]

Oktoberfest (München)
[ɔkˈtoːbɐˌfɛst]

Sächsische Schweiz (Sachsen)
[ˈzɛksɪʃə ʃvaɪ̯t͡s]

Zugspitze (Bayern)
[ˈt͡suːkˌʃpɪt͡sə]

# At the bakery

In der Bäckerei [ɪn deːɐ̯ ˌbɛkəˈʁaɪ̯]

das Vollkornbrot
[das ɔlkɔʁnˌbʁoːt]
wholemeal bread

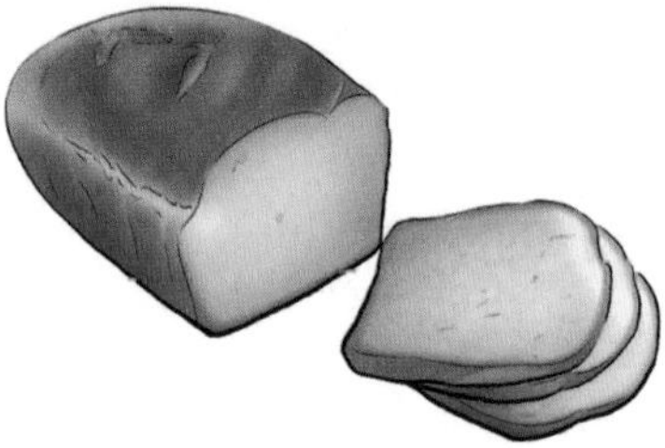

das Toastbrot
[das ˈtoːstˌbʁoːt]
white bread

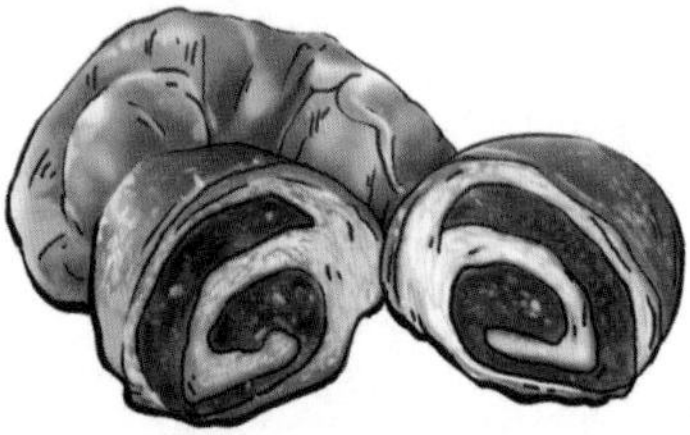

das Nusshörnchen
[das ˈnʊshœʁnçən]
hazelnut croissant

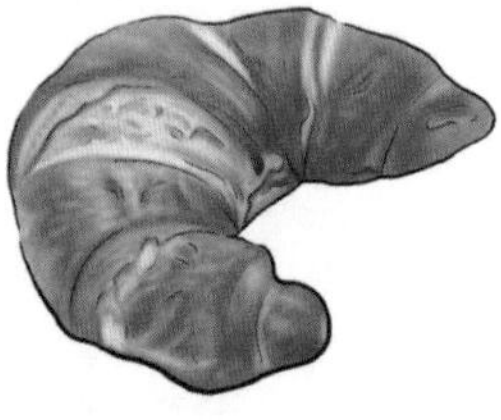

das Croissant
[das kʁo̯aˈsɑ̃ː]
croissant

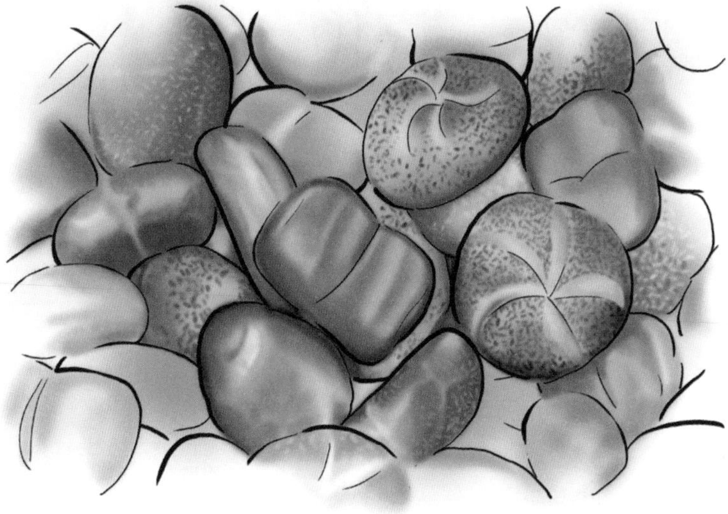

das Brötchen
[das ˈbʁøːtçən]

bun

das Baguette
[das baˈgɛt]

baguette

die Brezel
[diː ˈbʁeːt͡sl̩]

pretzel

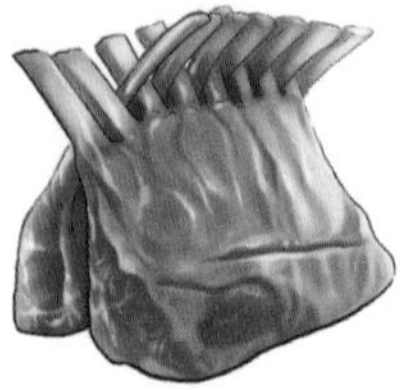

das Lammfleisch
[das ˈlamˌflaɪ̯ʃ]
lamb

das Kaninchen
[das kaˈniːnçən]
rabbit

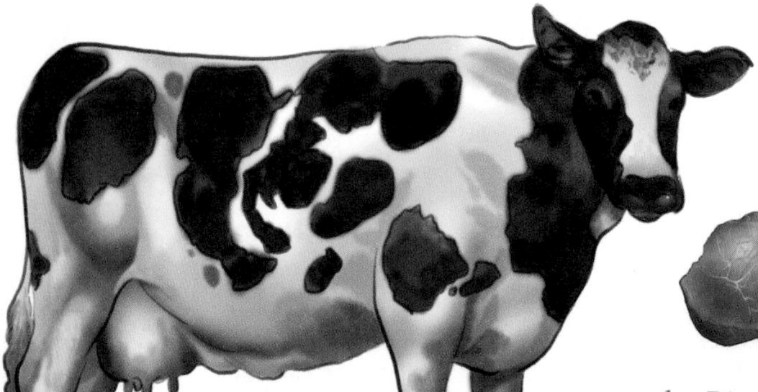

das Rindfleisch
[das ˈʁɪntˌflaɪ̯ʃ]
beef

# At the butchers

In der Metzgerei [ɪn deːɐ̯ mɛt͡sɡəˈʁaɪ̯]

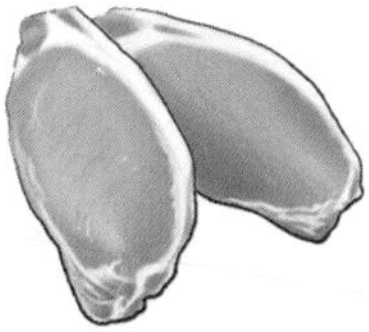

das Schweinefleisch
[das ˈʃvaɪ̯nəˌflaɪ̯ʃ]
pork

die Ente
[diː ˈɛntə]
duck

das Hühnerfleisch
[das ˈhyːnɐˌflaɪ̯ʃ]
chicken

# German sausages

Deutsche Wurstsorten ['dɔɪ̯ʧə 'vʊʁstˌzɔʁtn̩]

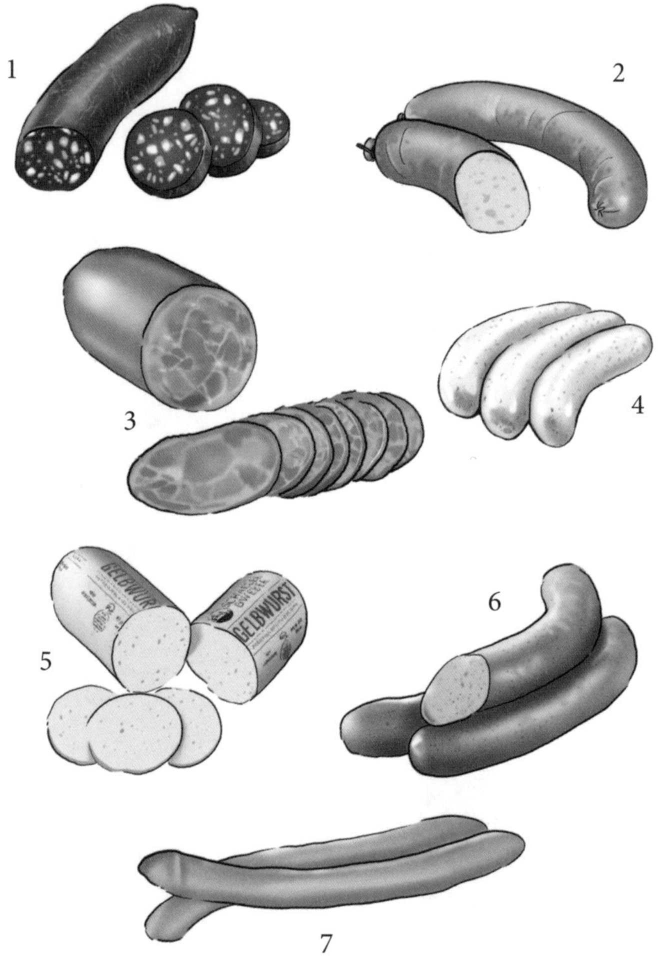
1
2
3
4
5
GELBWURST
GELBWURST
6
7

## (Hmm...Lecker!)

(Hmm... delicious!)

1. Blutwurst

[ˈbluːtˌvʊʁst] black pudding

2. Leberwurst

[ˈleːbɐˌvʊʁst] liver sausage

3. Schinken(wurst)

[ˈʃɪŋkn̩(vʊʁst)] ham

4. Weißwurst

[ˈvai̯sˌvʊʁst] Weisswurst

5. Gelbwurst

[ˈgɛlpˌvʊʁst] yellow sausage

6. Fleischwurst

[ˈflai̯ʃˌvʊʁst] pork sausage

7. Wiener Würstchen

[ˈviːnɐ ˈvʏʁstçən] Wiener sausage

**„Es ist mir Wurst.“**

[ɛs ɪst miːɐ̯ vʊʁst] I don't care.

# At the fishmongers

Im Fischgeschäft [ɪm fɪʃ geˈʃɛft]

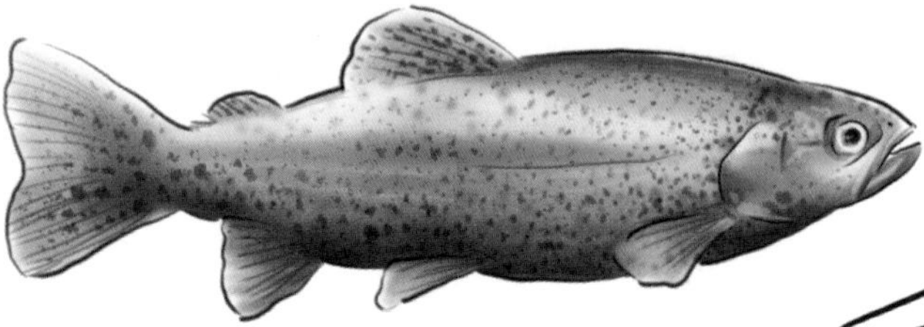

die Forelle
[diː ˌfoˈʁɛlə]
trout

der Fisch
[deːɐ̯ fɪʃ]
fish

die Krabbe
[diː ˈkʁabə]
crab

die Garnele
[diː gaʁˈneːlə]
shrimp

der Thunfisch
[deːɐ̯ ˈtuːnˌfɪʃ]
tuna

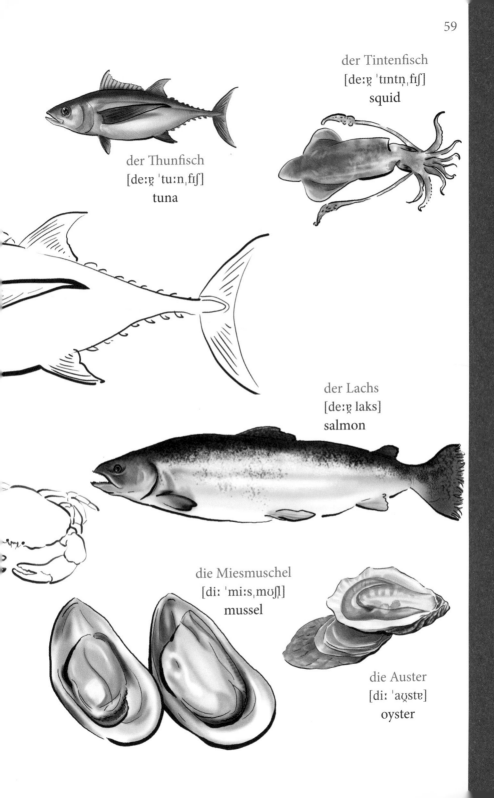

der Tintenfisch
[deːɐ̯ ˈtɪntn̩ˌfɪʃ]
squid

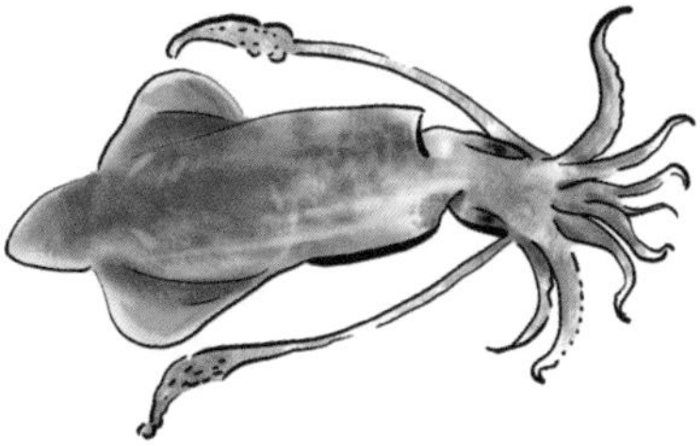

der Lachs
[deːɐ̯ laks]
salmon

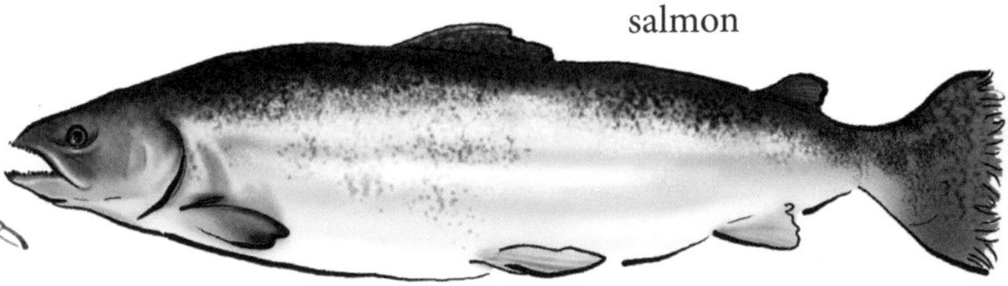

die Miesmuschel
[diː ˈmiːsˌmʊʃl̩]
mussel

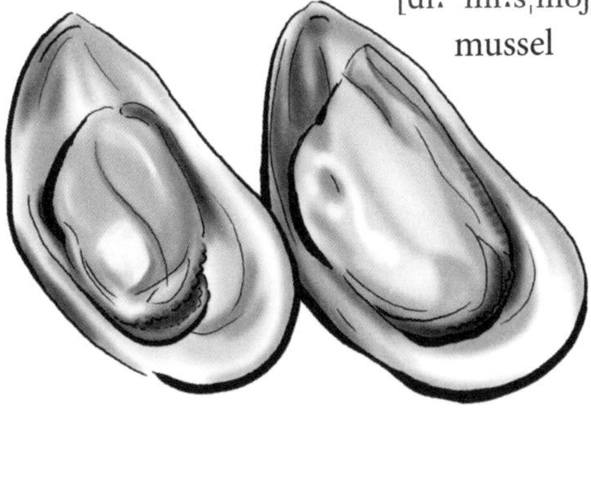

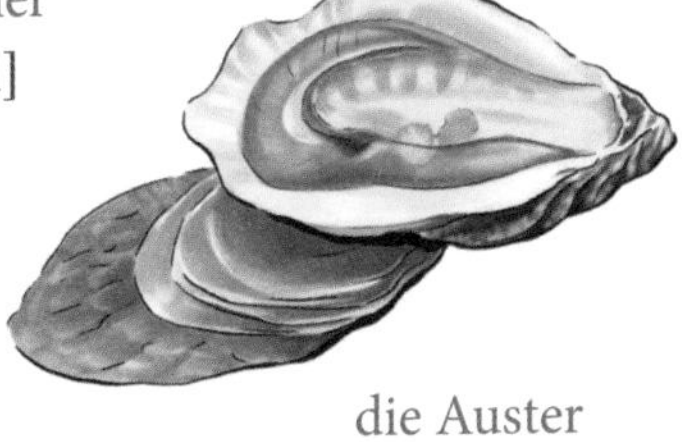

die Auster
[diː ˈaʊ̯stɐ]
oyster

1
2
3
4
5
6
7
8
9

# In the vegetable shop

Im Gemüseladen [ɪm gəˈmyːzəˌlaːdn̩]

1. die Aubergine
[diː obɛʁˈʒiːnə] aubergine

2. die Gurke
[diːˈɡʊʁkə] cucumber

3. der Brokkoli
[deːɐ̯ ˈbʁɔkoli] broccoli

4. die Artischocke
[diː aʁtiˈʃɔkə] artichoke

5. der Chinakohl
[deːɐ̯ çiːnaˌkoːl] chinese cabbage

6. die Erbsen
[diː ˈɛʁpsn̩] peas

7. der Blumenkohl
[deːɐ̯ bluːmənkoːl] cauliflower

8. die Möhre
[diː ˈmøːʁə] carrot

9. das Basilikum
[das baˈziːlikʊm] basil

1. der Ingwer
[deːɐ̯ ɪŋvɐ] ginger

2. der Kopfsalat
[deːɐ̯ ˈkɔp͡fzaˌlaːt] lettuce

3. der Kürbis
[deːɐ̯ ˈkʏʁbɪs] pumpkin

4. die Mandel
[diː [ˈmandl̩] almond

5. die Erdnuss
[diː eːɐ̯tnʊs] peanut

6. die Haselnuss
[diː ˈhaːzl̩ˌnʊs] hazelnut

7. der Knoblauch
[deːɐ̯ ˈknoːpˌlaʊ̯x] garlic

8. der Pilz
[deːɐ̯ pɪlt͡s] mushroom

9. die Kartoffel
[diː kaʳˈtɔf] potato

10. der Mais
[deːɐ̯ maɪ̯s] corn

11. die Walnuss
[diː ˈvalˌnʊs] walnut

1
2
3
4
7
5
6
8
9
10
11

1
2
3
4
5
6
7
8
9
10

1. die rote Beete
[diː ˈʁoːtə beːtə] beetroot

2. die Paprika
[diː ˈpapʁika] sweet pepper

3. die Zwiebel
[diː ˈt͡sviːbl̩] onion

4. der Weißkohl
[deːɐ̯ ˈvaɪ̯sˌkoːl] white cabbage

5. der Rotkohl
[deːɐ̯ ˈʁoːtkoːl] red cabbage

6. der Spargel
[deːɐ̯ ˈʃpaʁgl̩] asparagus

7. die Tomate
[diː toˈmaːtə] tomato

8. die Zucchini
[diː t͡sʊˈkiːni] courgette

9. der Sellerie
[deːɐ̯ ˈzɛləʁi] celery

10. der Spinat
[deːɐ̯ ʃpiˈnaːt] spinach

der Apfel
[deːɐ̯ ˈap͡fl̩]
apple

der grüne Apfel
[deːɐ̯ ˈɡʁyːnə ˈap͡fl̩]
green apple

die Birne
[diː ˈbɪʁnə]
pear

die Kirsche
[diː ˈkɪʁʃə]
cherry

die Pflaume
[diː ˈp͡flaʊ̯mə]
plum

die Olive
[diː oˈliːvə]
olive

die Kokosnuss
[diː ˈkoːkɔsˌnʊs]
coconut

die Erdbeere
[diː ˈeːɐ̯tbeːʁə]
strawberry

die Ananas
[diː ˈananas]
pineapple

der Granatapfel
[deːɐ̯ gʁaˈnaːtˌʔap͡fl̩]
pomegranate

die Brombeere
[diː ˈbʁɔmˌbeːʁə]
blackberry

die Himbeere
[diː ˈhɪmˌbeːʁə]
raspberry

# In the fruit shop

Im Obstladen [ɪm ˈoːpstˌlaːdn̩]

die Blaubeere
[diː blaʊ̯ˌbeːʁə]
blueberry

die schwarze Johannisbeere
[diː ˈʃvaʁt͡sə joˈhanɪsˌbeːʁə]
blackcurrant

die rote Johannisbeere
[diː ˈʁoːtə joˈhanɪsˌbeːʁə]
redcurrant

die Limette
[diː liˈmɛtə]
lime

die Zitrone
[diː siˈtʁoːnə]
lemon

die Avocado
[diː avoˈkaːdo]
avocado

die Stachelbeere
[diː ˈʃtaxl̩ˌbeːʁə]
gooseberry

der Pfirsich
[deːɐ̯ ˈp͡fɪʁzɪç]
peach

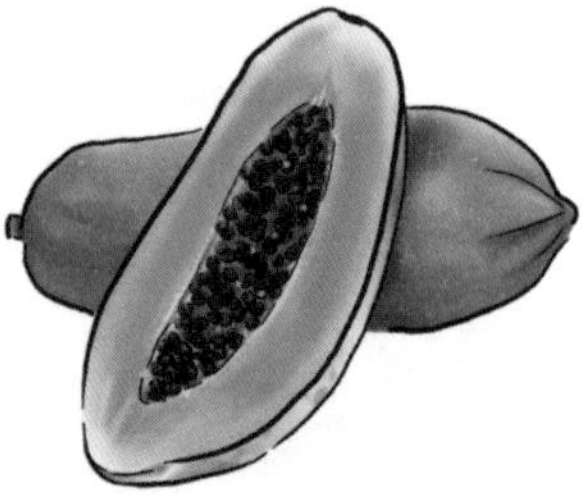

die Papaya
[diː paˈpaːja]
papaya

die Banane
[diː baˈnaːnə]
banana

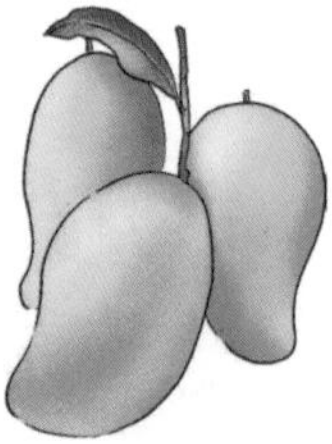

die Mango
[diː ˈmaŋgo]
mango

die Orange
[diː oˈʁɑ̃ːʒə]
orange

die Mandarine
[diː ˌmanda·ˈʁiːnə]
tangerine

die Wassermelone
[diː vasɐmeˌloːnə]
watermelon

die Weintraube
[diː ˈvaɪ̯nˌtʁaʊ̯bə]
grape

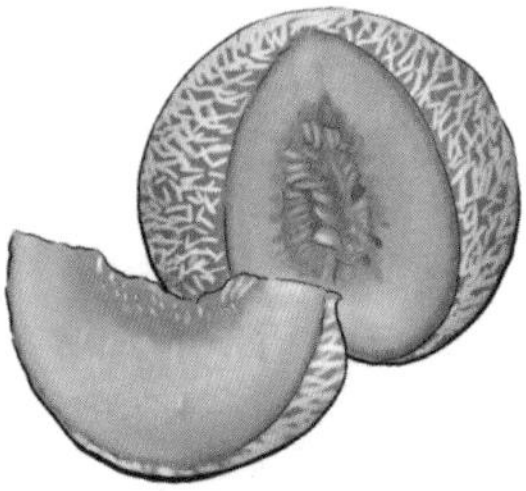

die Melone
[diː meˈloːnə]
melon

die Kiwi
[diː ˈkiːvi]
kiwi

# Beverages

Getränke [ɡəˈtʁɛŋkə]

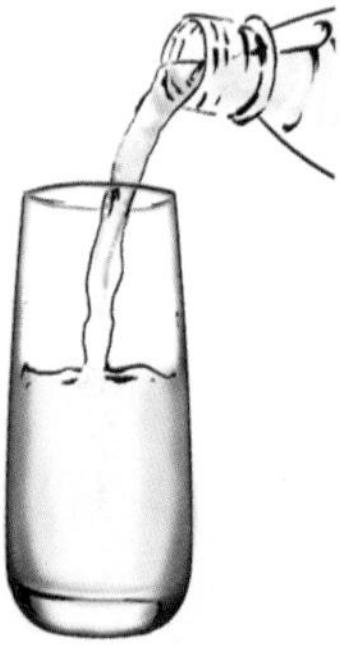

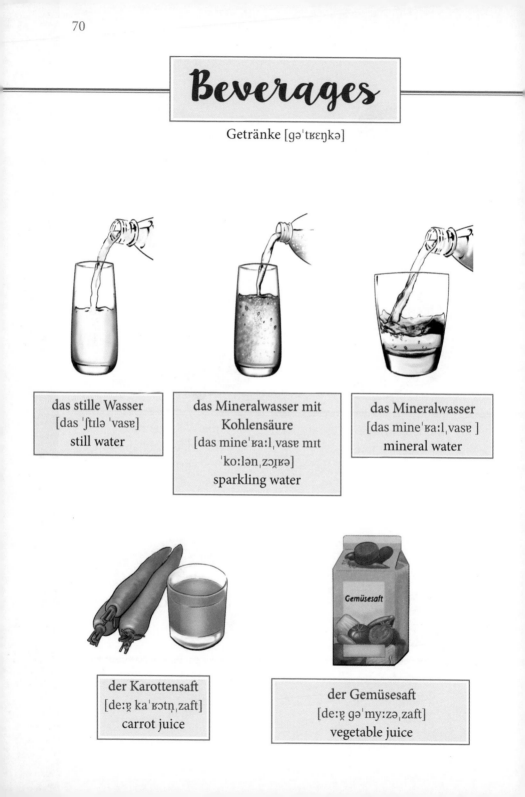

das stille Wasser
[das ˈʃtɪlə ˈvasɐ]
still water

das Mineralwasser mit Kohlensäure
[das mineˈʁaːlˌvasɐ mɪt ˈkoːlənˌzɔɪ̯ʁə]
sparkling water

das Mineralwasser
[das mineˈʁaːlˌvasɐ ]
mineral water

der Karottensaft
[deːɐ̯ kaˈʁɔtn̩ˌzaft]
carrot juice

Gemüsesaft

der Gemüsesaft
[deːɐ̯ ɡəˈmyːzəˌzaft]
vegetable juice

der Ananassaft
[deːɐ̯ ˈananasˌzaft]
pineapple juice

APFEL SCHORLE
APFEL SCHORLE

die Apfelsaftschorle
[diː ˈapflzaftˈʃɔʳlə]
apple juice spritzer

der Apfelsaft
[deːɐ̯ ˈapfl̩ˌzaft]
apple juice

der Orangensaft
[deːɐ̯ oˈʁãːʒn̩ˌzaft]
orange juice

der Traubensaft
[deːɐ̯ ˈtʁaʊ̯bn̩ˌzaft]
grape juice

der Tomatensaft
[deːɐ̯ toˈmaːtənzaft]
tomato juice

# At the bar

In der Bar [ɪn deːɐ̯ baːɐ̯]

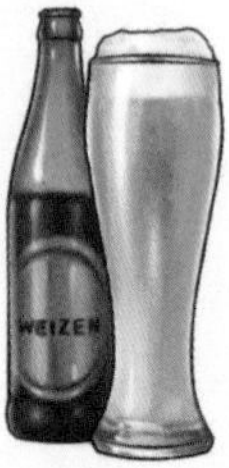
WEIZEN

das Bier
[das biːɐ̯]
beer

APPLE CIDER

der Apfelwein
[deːɐ̯ ˈap͡fl̩ˌvaɪ̯n]
apple cider

WHISKEY

der Whiskey
[deːɐ̯ ˈwɪski]
whisky

COGNAC

der Brandy
[deːɐ̯ ˈbʁɛndi]
brandy

der Rotwein
[deːɐ̯ ˈʁoːtˌvaɪ̯n]
red wine

der Weißwein
[deːɐ̯ ˈvaɪ̯sˌvaɪ̯n]
white wine

der Rosé
[deːɐ̯ ʁoˈzeː]
rosé wine

**Im Wein liegt die Wahrheit.**
[ɪm vaɪ̯n liːkt diː vaːɐ̯haɪ̯t] The truth is in the wine.

**Wein ist Poesie in Flaschen.**
[vaɪ̯n ɪst ˌpoeˈziː ɪn ˈflaʃən] Wine is poetry in a bottle.

**Auch weißer Wein macht eine rote Nase.**
[aʊ̯x ˈvaɪ̯sɐ vaɪ̯n maxt ˈaɪ̯nə ˈʁoːtə ˈnaːzə]
White wine can also make your nose red.

# Das Leben ist viel zu kurz, um schlechten Wein zu trinken.

[das ˈleːbn̩ ɪst fiːl t͡suː kʊʁt͡s ʊm ˈʃlɛçtn̩ vai̯n t͡suː ˈtrɪŋkŋ̍]

Life is too short to drink bad wine.

Johann Wolfgang von Goethe

ESPRESSO

Espresso

MILCHSCHAUM
ESPRESSO

Espresso macchiato

Filterkaffee

Filterkaffee

Ice Cream
ESPRESSO

Espresso mit Vanilleeis

# At the coffee shop

Im Café [ɪm kaˈfeː]

Espresso
[ˌɛsˈpʁɛso] espresso

Espresso macchiato
[ˌɛsˈpʁɛso makˈkiaːto] espresso macchiato

Filterkaffee
[ˈfɪltɐˌkafeː] filtered coffee

Espresso mit Vanilleeis [ˌɛsˈpʁɛso mɪt vaˈnɪləˌʔai̯s]
coffee Affogato

MILCHSCHAUM
ESPRESSO
AUFGESCHÄUMTE MILCH
MILCHSCHAUM
ESPRESSO
AUFGESCHÄUMTE MILCH
ESPRESSO
AUFGESCHÄUMTE MILCH

Milchkaffee Cappuccino Latte macchiato

heiße Schokolade heiße Milch

Milchkaffee
[ˈmɪlçkaˌfeː] milk coffee

Cappuccino
[ˌkapʊˈtʃiːno] cappuccino

Latte macchiato
[ˈlatə maˌki̯aːto] latte macchiato

heiße Schokolade
[ˈhai̯sə ʃokoˈlaːdə] hot chocolate

heiße Milch
[ˈhai̯sə mɪlç] hot milk

1

2

3

# Tea

Tee [teː]

4

5

6

1. der schwarze Tee

[deːɐ̯ ˈʃvaʁt͡sə teː] black tea

2. der weiße Tee

[deːɐ̯ ˈvaɪ̯sə teː] white tea

3. der grüne Tee

[deːɐ̯ ˈɡʁyːnə teː] green tea

4. der Früchtetee

[deːɐ̯ ˈfʁʏçtəˌteː] fruit tea

5. der Roibuschtee

[deːɐ̯ ˈʁɔɪ̯bʊʃˌteː] rooibos tea

6. der Kräutertee

[deːɐ̯ ˈkʁɔɪ̯tɐˌteː] herbal tea

**Entschuldigung!**
**Ich würde gern bestellen.**

[ɛntˈʃʊldɪɡʊŋ ɪç ˈvʏʁdə ɡɛʁn bəˈʃtɛlən]

Excuse me, I would like to order, please.

**Welche Spezialitäten gibt es aus dieser Region?**

[ˈvɛlçə ʃpet͡si̯aliˈtɛːtn ɡiːpt ɛs aʊ̯s ˈdiːzɐ ʁeˈɡi̯oːn̩]

What is the specialty of this region?

# In the restaurant

Im Restaurant [ɪm ʁɛsto'ʁɑ̃ː]

## das Restaurant / die Gaststätte

[das ʁɛsto'ʁɑ̃ː/ diː 'ɡastˌʃtɛtə] restaurant

## die Speisekarte

[diː 'ʃpai̯zəˌkaʁtə] menu

## die Vorspeise

[diː 'foːɐ̯ʃpai̯zə] starter

## das Hauptgericht

[das 'hau̯ptɡəˌʁɪçt] main course

## der Nachtisch

[deːɐ̯ 'naːxˌtɪʃ] dessert

| | |
|---|---|
| Haben Sie einen Tisch für zwei Personen?<br>['haːbn̩ ziː 'ai̯nən tɪʃ fyːɐ̯ t͡svai̯ pɛʁ'zoːnən] | Do you have a table for two? |
| Gibt es ein Tagesmenü?<br>[giːpt ɛs ai̯n 'taːɡəs me'nyː] | What is today's special? |
| Was können Sie mir empfehlen?<br>[vas 'kœnən ziː miːɐ̯ ɛm'p͡feːlən] | What would you recommend? |
| Ich hätte gern...<br>[ɪç 'hɛtə ɡɛʁn] | I would like… |

1. die Vorspeisengabel [diː ˈfoːɐ̯ʃpaɪ̯zn̩ˈɡaːbl̩]
   salad fork
2. die Gabel [diː ˈɡaːbl̩]
   dinner fork
3. das Messer [das ˈmɛsɐ]
   dinner knife
4. das Vorspeisenmesser [das ˈfoːɐ̯ʃpaɪ̯znˈmɛsɐ]
   salad knife
5. der Suppenlöffel [deːɐ̯ ˈzʊpn̩ˌlœfl̩]
   soup spoon
6. das Buttermesser [das ˈbʊtɐˌmɛsɐ]
   butter knife
7. die Kuchengabel [diː ˈkuːxn̩ˌɡaːbl̩]
   dessert fork
8. der Kaffeelöffel [deːɐ̯ ˈkafeˌlœfl̩]
   coffee spoon
9. der Brotteller [deːɐ̯ bʁoːtˈtɛlɐ]
   bread plate
10. der Teller [deːɐ̯ ˈtɛlɐ]
   main plate
11. das Wasserglas [das ˈvasɐˌɡlaːs]
   water glass
12. das Rotweinglas [das ˈʁoːtvaɪ̯nˌɡlaːs]
   red wine glass
13. das Weißweinglas [das ˈvaɪ̯svaɪ̯nˌɡlaːs]
   white wine glass

6
8
7
9
1
2
10

# Formal table setting

Der gedeckte Tisch [deːɐ̯ ɡəˈdɛktə tɪʃ]

11
12
13
3
4
5

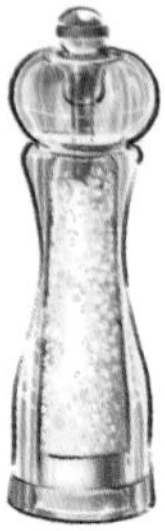

der Pfeffer
[deːɐ̯ [ˈp͡fɛfɐ]
pepper

das Salz
[das zal͡t͡s]
salt

# Seasonings

Die Gewürze [diː ˌɡəˈvʏʁt͡sə]

CURRY
PULVER

das Chilipulver
[das ˈt͡ʃiːliˌpʊlfɐ]
chili powder

das Pesto
[das ˈpɛsto]
pesto

das Currypulver
[das ˈkœʁiˌpʊlfɐ]
curry powder

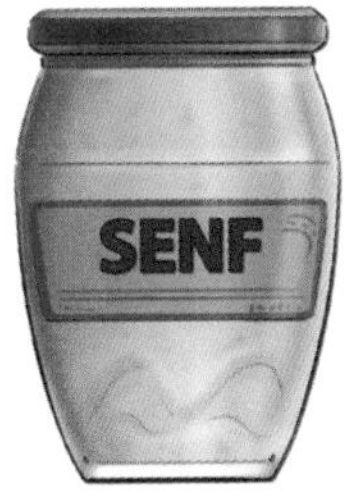
SENF

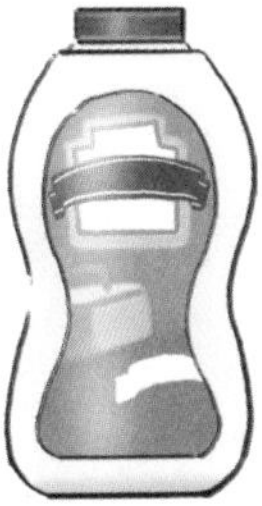

der Senf
[deːɐ̯ zɛnf]
mustard

das Tomatenketchup
[das toˈmaːtn̩ˈkɛtʃəp]
tomato sauce

die Mayonnaise
[diː majɔˈnɛːzə]
mayonnaise

Süßstoff

der Zucker
[deːɐ̯ ˈt͡sʊkɐ]
sugar

der Süßstoff
[deːɐ̯ ˈsyːsˌʃtɔf]
sweetener

PAPRIKA

PARMESAN

das Paprikapulver
[das ˈpapʁikaˌpʊlfɐ]
paprika powder

der Parmesankäse
[deːɐ̯ paʁmeˈzaːnˌkɛːzə]
parmesan

die Sojasoße
[diː ˈzoːjaˌzoːsə]
soy sauce

| | |
|---|---|
| die Mahlzeit<br>[diː ˈmaːlˌt͡saɪ̯t] | meal |
| das Frühstück<br>[das ˈfʁyːˌʃtʏk] | breakfast |
| das Mittagessen<br>[das ˈmɪtaːkˌʔɛsn̩] | lunch |
| das Abendessen<br>[das ˈaːbn̩tˌʔɛsn̩] | dinner |

**Guten Appetit!**

[ˌɡutən ˌʔapəˈtit]

Enjoy your meal!

## Die Rechnung, bitte.

[diː ˈʁɛçnʊŋ ˈbɪtə]

May I have the bill, please?

Das Essen war sehr gut! — The food was very good!
[das ˈɛsn̩ vaːɐ̯ zeːɐ̯ guːt]

Köstlich! — Delicious!
[ˈkœstlɪç]

Stimmt so. — Keep the change.
[ʃtɪmt zoː]

das Trinkgeld — tip
[das ˈtʁɪŋkˌgɛlt]

Erdnussmus fein

die Erdbeermarmelade
[diː ˈeːɐ̯tbeːɐ̯maʁməˌlaːdə]
strawberry jam

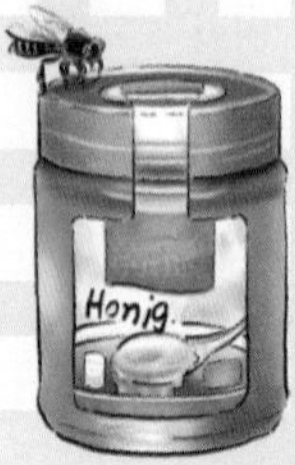
Honig

der Honig
[deːɐ̯ ˈhoːnɪç]
honey

die Erdnussbutter
[diː ˈeːɐ̯tnʊsˌbʊtɐ]
peanut butter

Marmelade

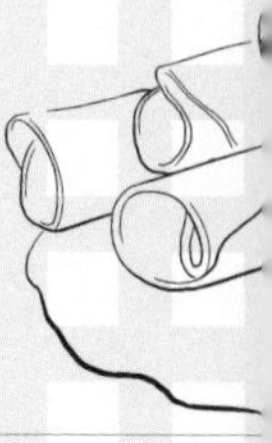

marmelade

die Butter
[diː ˈbʊtɐ]
butter

die Orangenmarmelade
[diː oˈʁɑ̃ːʒn̩maʁməˌlaːdə]
orange marmalade

das gekochte Ei
[das ɡəˈkɔxtə aɪ̯]
soft-boiled egg

der Toast
[deːɐ̯ toːst]
toast

das Omelett
[das ɔmˈlɛt]
omelette

# Breakfast

Das Frühstück [das ˈfʁyːˌʃtʏk]

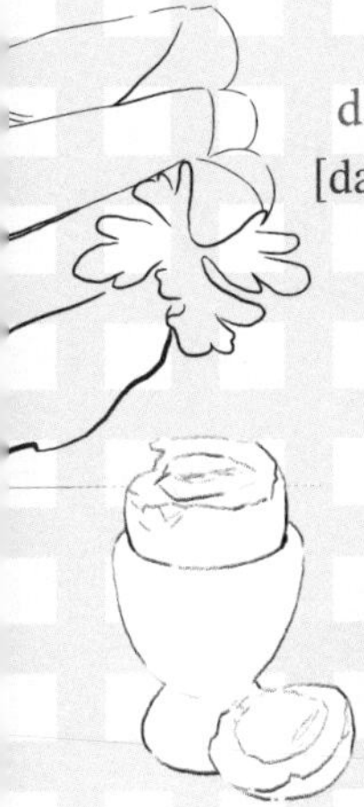

das Müsli
[das ˈmyːsli]
muesli

der Obstsalat
[deːɐ̯ ˈoːpstzaˌlaːt]
fruit salad

der Joghurt
[deːɐ̯ ˈjoːɡʊʁt]
yogurt

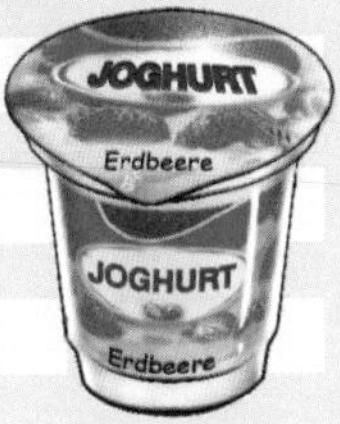
JOGHURT
Erdbeere
JOGHURT
Erdbeere

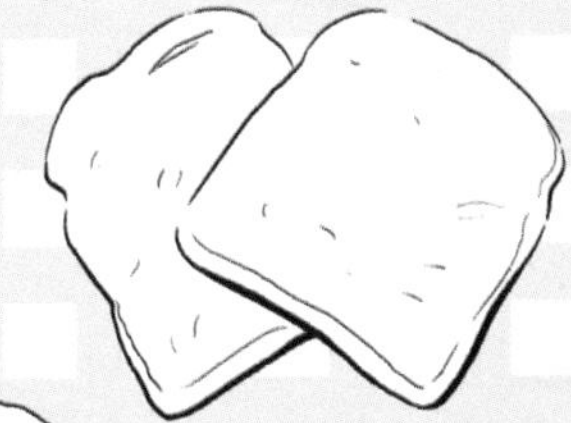

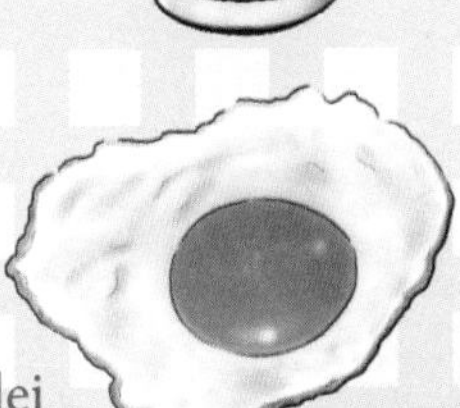

das Spiegelei
[das ˈʃpiːɡl̩ˌʔaɪ̯]
fried egg

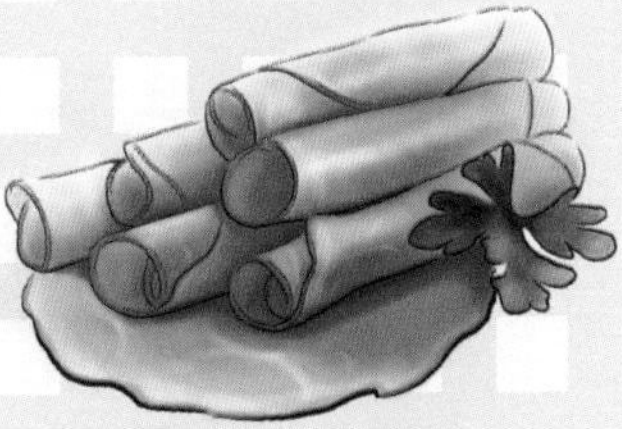

der Schinken
[deːɐ̯ ˈʃɪŋkn̩]
ham

das Rührei
[das ˈʁyːɐ̯ˌʔaɪ̯]
scrambled eggs

die Frikadellen mit Gemüse
[diː fʁikaˈdɛlən mɪt ɡəˈmyːzə]
meatballs with vegetables

das Schnitzel mit Pommes Frites
[das ˈʃnɪt͡sl̩ mɪt pɔmˈfʁɪt]
escalope with chips

das Steak
[das steːk]
steak

das Eisbein mit Sauerkraut
[das aɪ̯sˌbaɪ̯n mɪt ˈzaʊ̯ɐˌkʁaʊ̯t]
leg of pork with sauerkraut

# Main course

Das Hauptgericht [das ˈhau̯ptɡəˌʁɪçt]

die Schweinshaxe
[diː ʃvai̯nsˈhaksə]
pork knuckle

der Gemüseauflauf
[deːɐ̯ ɡəˈmyːzə ˈau̯fˌlau̯f]
vegetable bake

die Kohlrouladen
[diː ˈkoːlʁuˌlaːdn̩]
stuffed cabbages

# Side dishes

Die Beilagen [diː ˈbai̯laːgən]

die Pommes Frites
[diː pɔmˈfʁɪt]
chips

die gebackenen Kartoffeln
[diː gəˈbakənən kaʁˈtɔfl̩n]
roast potatoes

das Kartoffelpüree
[das kaʁˈtɔfl̩pyˌʁeː]
mashed potatoes

der Salat
[deːɐ̯ zaˈlaːt]
salad

das Rotkraut
[das ˈʁoːtkʁaʊ̯t]
red cabbage

das Sauerkraut
[das ˈzaʊ̯ɐˌkʁaʊ̯t]
pickled cabbage

# Snack

der Imbiss [deːɐ̯ ɪmbɪs]

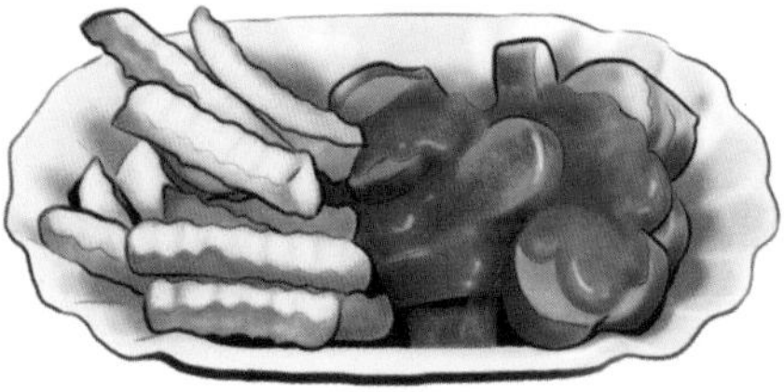

die Currywurst
[diː ˈkœʁiˌvʊʁst]

curry sausage

die gebratenen Nudeln
[diː ɡəˈbʁaːtənən ˈnuːdl̩n]

fried noodles

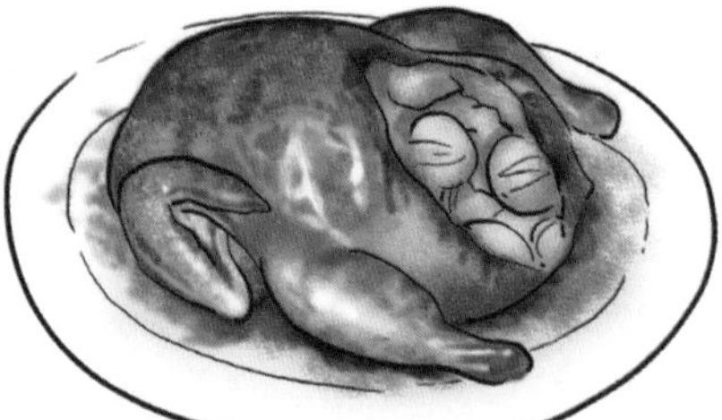

das gebratene Hühnchen
[das ɡəˈbʁaːtənə ˈhyːnçən]

roasted chicken

der Dönerkebab

[deːɐ̯ ˈdøːnɐˌkeːbap]

doner kebab

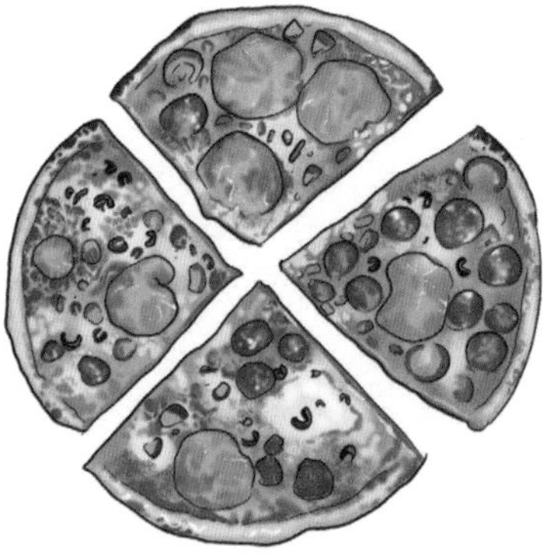

die Pizza

[diː ˈpɪt͡sa]

pizza

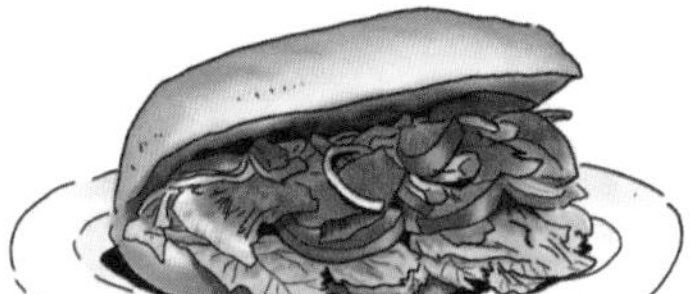

das Sandwich

[das ˈzɛntvɪt͡ʃ]

sandwich

# Dessert

Die Süßspeisen [diː ˈzyːsˌʃpaɪ̯zn̩]

1. Mandel-Pfirsich Kuchen [ˈmandl̩ ˈp͡fɪʁzɪç ˈkuːxn̩]

• • •

2. Aprikosenkuchen [ˌapʁiˈkoːzn̩ˈkuːxn̩]

• • •

3. Apfelstrudel [ˈap͡fl̩ˌʃtʁuːdl̩]

• • •

4. Bienenstich [biːnənˌʃtɪç]

• • •

5. Schwarzwälder Kirschtorte [ˈʃvaʁtsˌvɛldɐ ˈkɪʁʃˌtɔʁtə]

• • •

6. Zwetschgen-Käse Kuchen [ˈt͡svɛt͡ʃgən ˈkɛːzə ˈkuːxn̩]

• • •

7. Erdbeerkuchen [ˈeːɐ̯tbeːɐ̯ˌkuːxn̩]

• • •

8. Pflaumenkuchen [ˈp͡flaʊ̯mənˌkuːxn̩]

• • •

9. Rhabarber-Baiser Kuchen [ʁaˈbaʁbɐ bɛˈzeː ˈkuːxn̩]

• • •

10 . Marzipan-Schnecken [ˈmaʁt͡sipaːn [ˈʃnɛkn̩]

• • •

11. Kaiserschmarren [ˈkaɪ̯zɐˌʃmaʁən]

1

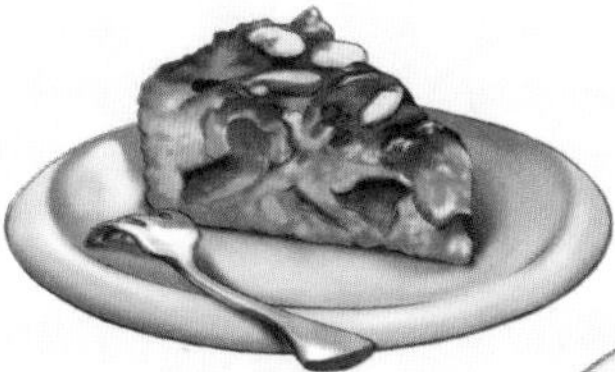

2

3

6

4

5

9

7

8

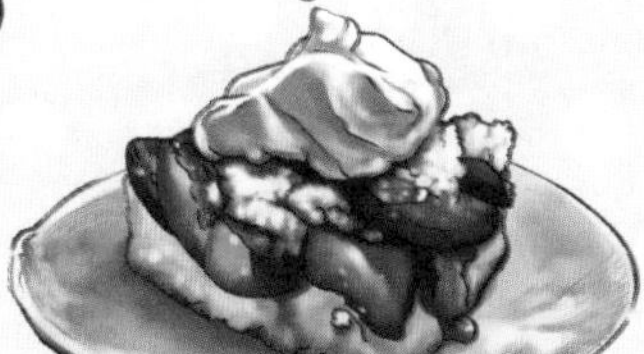

10

11

# Places to shop

Einkaufsmöglichkeiten [ˈaɪ̯nkaʊ̯fsˌmøːklɪçkaɪ̯tn̩]

REWE

NORMA

ALDI

EDEKA

KAUFLAND

PENNY

LIDL

NETTO

# das Einkaufszentrum
[das ˈaɪ̯nkaʊ̯fsˌt͡sɛntʁʊm] shopping centre

# das Kaufhaus
[das ˈkaʊ̯fˌhaʊ̯s] department store

# der Markt
[deːɐ̯ maʁkt] market

# der Supermarkt
[deːɐ̯ ˈzuːpɐˌmaʁkt] supermarket

# der Laden
[deːɐ̯ ˈlaːdn̩] shop

# der Bioladen
[deːɐ̯ ˈbiːolaːdn̩] organic food shop

# Everything your heart desires

Alles, was das Herz begehrt [ˈaləs vas das hɛʁt͡s bəˈgeːɐ̯t]

die Parfümerie
[diː paʁfyməˈʁiː]
cosmetics shop

der Friseursalon
[deːɐ̯ fʁiˈzøːɐ̯zaˌloːn]
hair salon

das Juweliergeschäft
[das juveˈliːɐ̯ˌgəˈʃɛft̰]
jewellery shop

der Blumenladen
[deːɐ ˈbluːməˈlaːdn]
flower shop

die Modeboutique
[diː ˈmoːdəbu.tik]
fashion boutique

---

das Schuhgeschäft
[das ˈʃuːgəˌʃɛft]
shoe shop

---

der Souvenirladen
[deːɐ̯ zuvəˈniːɐ̯ˌlaːdn̩]
souvenir shop

---

das Antiquitätengeschäft
[das antikviˈtɛːtn̩gəˌʃɛft]
antique shop

---

| | |
|---|---|
| Ich möchte...<br>[ɪç ˈmœçtə] | I would like… |
| ein Hemd.<br>[ai̯n hɛmt] | a shirt. |
| eine Hose.<br>[ai̯nə ˈhoːzə] | a pair of trousers. |
| ein Paar Schuhe.<br>[ai̯n paːɐ̯ ˈʃuːə] | a pair of shoes. |
| ein Paar Strümpfe.<br>[ai̯n paːɐ̯ ˈʃtʁʏmp͡fə] | a pair of socks. |
| zwei Blusen.<br>[t͡svai̯ ˈbluːzən] | two blouses. |
| drei Jacken.<br>[dʁai̯ ˈjakən] | three jackets. |
| vier Röcke.<br>[fiːɐ̯ ˈʁœkə] | four skirts. |
| fünf Mäntel.<br>[fʏnf ˈmɛntəl] | five coats. |

| | |
|---|---|
| Wie viel kostet das?<br>[viː fiːl ˈkoːstət das] | How much does it cost? |
| Das kostet...Euro.<br>[das ˈkoːstət ˈɔʏ̯ʁo] | It costs…euros. |
| Das ist sehr teuer.<br>[das ɪst zeːɐ̯ ˈtɔʏ̯ɐ] | That is very expensive. |
| Können Sie mir das günstiger verkaufen?<br>[ˈkœnən ziː miːɐ̯ das ˈɡʏnstɪɡɐ fɛɐ̯ˈkaʊ̯fn̩] | Can you do better on price? |
| Das ist sehr billig.<br>[das ɪst zeːɐ̯ ˈbɪlɪç] | That is very cheap. |
| Danke, das ist genug.<br>[ˈdaŋkə das ɪst ɡəˈnuːk] | No more, thanks. |
| Der Preis ist angemessen.<br>[deːɐ̯ pʁaɪ̯s ɪst ˈanɡəˌmɛsn̩] | The price is reasonable. |
| Das ist zu kurz / zu lang.<br>[das ɪst t͡suː kʊʁt͡s t͡suː laŋ] | It's too short / too long. |
| Das ist zu weit / eng.<br>[das ɪst t͡suː vaɪ̯t t͡suː ɛŋ] | It's too loose / too tight. |

**Kann ich das anprobieren?**

[kan ɪç das ˈanpʁoˌbiːʁən]

May I try it on?

**Wo ist die Umkleidekabine?**

[voː ɪst diː ˈʊmklaɪ̯dəkaˌbiːnə]

Where is the fitting room?

# Rabatt

[ʁaˈbat]
discount

# Ermäßigter Preis

[ɛɐ̯ˈmɛːsɪçtə pʁaɪ̯s]
at a reduced price

# Sonderangebot

[ˈzɔndɐ|angəboːt]
on sale

# Werbeaktion

[ˈvɛʁbəakˈt͡si̯oːn]
promotion

# Colours

Die Farben [diː ˈfaʁbən]

**weiß**
[vai̯s]
white

**schwarz**
[ʃvaʁt͡s]
black

**orange**
[oˈʁɑ̃ːʒə]
orange

**braun**
[bʁau̯n]
brown

**grau**
[ɡʁau̯]
grey

**hellblau**
[ˈhɛlˌblau̯]
light blue

hell
[hɛl]
light

dunkel
[ˈdʊŋkl̩]
dark

rot
[ʁoːt]
red

rosa
[ˈʁoːza]
pink

gelb
[gɛlp]
yellow

grün
[gʁyːn]
green

dunkelblau
[ˈdʊŋkəlˌblaʊ̯]
dark blue

lila
[ˈliːla]
purple

# Numbers

Die Zahlen [diː ˈt͡saːlən]

| | | |
|---|---|---|
| 0 | null | [nʊl] |
| 1 | eins | [aɪ̯ns] |
| 2 | zwei | [t͡svaɪ̯] |
| 3 | drei | [dʁaɪ̯] |
| 4 | vier | [fiːɐ̯] |
| 5 | fünf | [fʏnf] |
| 6 | sechs | [zɛks] |
| 7 | sieben | [ˈziːbn̩] |
| 8 | acht | [axt] |
| 9 | neun | [nɔɪ̯n] |
| 10 | zehn | [t͡seːn] |
| 11 | elf | [ɛlf] |
| 12 | zwölf | [t͡svœlf] |
| 13 | dreizehn | [ˈdʁaɪ̯t͡seːn] |
| 14 | vierzehn | [ˈfɪʁt͡seːn] |
| 15 | fünfzehn | [ˈfʏnft͡seːn] |
| 16 | sechzehn | [ˈzɛçt͡seːn] |
| 17 | siebzehn | [ˈziːpʦeːn] |
| 18 | achtzehn | [ˈaxt͡seːn] |
| 19 | neunzehn | [ˈnɔɪ̯nt͡seːn] |
| 20 | zwanzig | [ˈt͡svant͡sɪç] |
| 21 | einundzwanzig | [ˌaɪ̯nʊntˈt͡svant͡sɪç] |
| 22 | zweiundzwanzig | [ˌt͡svaɪ̯ʊntˈt͡svant͡sɪç] |
| 23 | dreiundzwanzig | [ˌdʁaɪ̯ʊntˈt͡svant͡sɪç] |
| 24 | vierundzwanzig | [ˌfiːɐ̯ʊntˈt͡svant͡sɪç] |
| 25 | fünfundzwanzig | [ˌfʏnfʊntˈt͡svant͡sɪç] |
| 26 | sechsundzwanzig | [ˌzɛksʊntˈt͡svant͡sɪç] |

| | | |
|---|---|---|
| 27 | siebenundzwanzig | [ˈziːbn̩ʊntˈt͡svant͡sɪç] |
| 28 | achtundzwanzig | [ˌaxtʊntˈt͡svant͡sɪç] |
| 29 | neunundzwanzig | [ˌnɔɪ̯nʊntˈt͡svant͡sɪç] |
| 30 | dreißig | [ˈdʁaɪ̯sɪç] |
| 40 | vierzig | [ˈfɪʁt͡sɪç] |
| 50 | fünfzig | [ˈfʏnft͡sɪç] |
| 60 | sechzig | [ˈzɛçt͡sɪç] |
| 70 | siebzig | [ˈziːpt͡sɪç] |
| 80 | achtzig | [ˈaxt͡sɪç] |
| 90 | neunzig | [ˈnɔɪ̯nt͡sɪç] |
| 100 | hundert | [ˈhʊndɐt] |
| 101 | hunderteins | [ˈhʊndɐtaɪ̯ns] |
| 102 | hundertzwei | [ˈhʊndɐtˌt͡svaɪ̯] |
| 200 | zweihundert | [ˈt͡svaɪ̯ˌhʊndɐt] |
| 300 | dreihundert | [ˈdʁaɪ̯ˌhʊndɐt] |
| 400 | vierhundert | [ˈfiːɐ̯ˌhʊndɐt] |
| 500 | fünfhundert | [ˈfʏnfˈhʊndɐt] |
| 600 | sechshundert | [zɛksˈhʊndɐt] |
| 700 | siebenhundert | [ˈziːbn̩ˈhʊndɐt] |
| 800 | achthundert | [ˈaxtˌhʊndɐt] |
| 900 | neunhundert | [nɔɪ̯nˈhʊndɐt] |
| 1000 | tausend | [ˈtaʊ̯zn̩t] |
| 10 000 | zehntausend | [tseːntaʊ̯zn̩t] |
| 100 000 | hunderttausend | [ˌhʊndɐtˈtaʊ̯zn̩t] |
| 1 000 000 | eine Million | [ˈaɪ̯nə mɪˈli̯oːn] |

**1**

**erster**

['eːɐ̯stɐ]

first

**2**

**zweiter**

['t͡svaɪ̯tɐ]

second

**3**

**dritter**

['dʁɪtɐ]

third

| | | |
|---|---|---|
| vierter | [ˈfiːɐ̯tɐ] | fourth |
| fünfter | [ˈfʏnftɐ] | fifth |
| sechster | [ˈzɛkstɐ] | sixth |
| siebter | [ˈziːptɐ] | seventh |
| achter | [ˈaxtɐ] | eighth |
| neunter | [ˈnɔɪ̯ntɐ] | ninth |
| zehnter | [ˈt͡seːntɐ] | tenth |

# When then?

Wann denn? [van dɛn]

## gestern

[ˈgɛstɐn]

yesterday

## gestern Abend

[ˈgɛstɐn ˈaː.bənt]

yesterday evening

## vorgestern

[ˈfoːɐ̯gɛstɐn]

the day before yesterday

## letzte Woche

[ˈlɛt͡stə ˈvɔxə]

last week

## letztes Jahr

[ˈlɛtstəs jaːɐ̯]

last year

## heute

[ˈhɔɪ̯tə]

today

## morgen

[ˈmɔʁgn̩]

tomorrow

## übermorgen

[ˈyːbɐmɔʁgən]

the day after tomorrow

## nächste Woche

[ˈnɛːçstə ˈvɔxə]

next week

## nächstes Jahr

[ˈnɛːçstəs jaːɐ̯]

next year

# All about time

Rund um die Uhr [ʁʊnt ʊm diː uːɐ̯]

| | | |
|---|---|---|
| die Uhrzeit | [diː ˈuːɐ̯ˌt͡sa͜ɪt] | time |
| die Uhr | [diː uːɐ̯] | clock |
| die Sekunde | [diː zeˈkʊndə] | second |
| die Sekunden | [diː zeˈkʊndn̩] | seconds |
| die Minute | [diː miˈnuːtə] | minute |
| die Minuten | [diː miˈnuːtən] | minutes |
| ein Viertel | [a͜ɪn ˈfɪʳtl̩] | quarter of an hour |
| die halbe Stunde | [diː ˈhalbə ˈʃtʊndə] | half an hour |
| die Stunde | [diː ˈʃtʊndə] | hour |
| die Stunden | [diː ˈʃtʊndən] | hours |

der Morgen

[deːɐ̯ ˈmɔʳgŋ̍]

morning

der Mittag

[deːɐ̯ ˈmɪtaːk]

noon

der Nachmittag

[deːɐ̯ ˈnaːxmɪˌtaːk]

afternoon

der Abend

[deːɐ̯ ˈaːbn̩t]

evening

die Nacht

[diː naxt]

night

die Mitternacht

[diː ˈmɪtɐˌnaxt]

midnight

früh

[fʁyː]

early

spät

[ʃpɛːt]

late

## Wie spät ist es?

[viː ʃpɛːt ɪst ɛs]

What time is it?

12
1
2
3
4
5
6
7
8
9
10
11

7:10 Uhr
Es ist zehn nach sieben.
[ɛs ɪst t͡seːn naːx ˈziːbn̩]
It’s ten past seven.

**Es ist ein Uhr.**

[ɛs ɪst a͡ɪn uːɐ̯]

It’s one a.m.

7:15 Uhr
Es ist Viertel nach sieben.
[ɛs ɪst ˈfɪʳtl̩ naːx ˈziːbn̩]
It’s a quarter past seven.

8:00 Uhr
Es ist acht Uhr.
[ɛs ɪst axt uːɐ]
It’s eight a.m.

9:50 Uhr
Es ist zehn vor zehn.
[ɛs ɪst ʦeːn t͡seːn foːɐ̯ t͡seːn]
It's ten to ten.

10:00 Uhr
Es ist zehn Uhr.
[ɛs ɪst t͡seːn uːɐ̯]
It's ten a.m.

10:10 Uhr
Es ist zehn nach zehn.
[ɛs ɪst ʦeːn t͡seːn naːx t͡seːn]
It's ten past ten.

10:30 Uhr
Es ist halb elf.
[ɛs ɪst halp ɛlf]
It's half past ten.

12:00 Uhr
Es ist Mittag.
[ɛs ɪst ˈmɪtaːk]
It's midday.

19:55 Uhr
Es ist fünf vor acht Uhr abends.
[ɛs ɪst fʏnf foːɐ̯ axt uːɐ̯ ˈaːbn̩t͡s]
It's five to eight.

22:00 hrs.
Es ist zehn Uhr abends.
[ɛs ɪst t͡seːn uːɐ̯ ˈaːbn̩t͡s]
It's ten p.m.

00:00 hrs.
Es ist Mitternacht.
[ɛs ɪst ˈmɪtɐˌnaxt]
It's midnight.

# Seven days of the week

Die Wochentage
[diː ˈvɔxn̩ˌtaːɡə]

| Sonntag ['zɔnˌtaːk] | Montag ['moːnˌtaːk] | Dienstag ['diːnsˌtaːk] |
|---|---|---|
| Sunday | Monday | Tuesday |

der Werktag
[deːɐ̯ ˈvɛʁkˌtaːk]
work day

das Wochenende
[das ˈvɔxn̩ˌʔɛndə]
weekend

der Feiertag
[deːɐ̯ ˈfaɪ̯ɐˌtaːk]
holiday

der Ruhetag
[deːɐ̯ ˈʁuːəˌtaːk]
rest day

| Mittwoch | Donnerstag | Freitag | Samstag |
|---|---|---|---|
| [ˈmɪtˌvɔx] | [ˈdɔnɐsˌtaːk] | [ˈfʁaɪ̯taːk] | [ˈzamstaːk] |
| Wednesday | Thursday | Friday | Saturday |

| | |
|---|---|
| Welchen Tag haben wir heute?<br>[ˈvɛlçn̩ taːk ˈhaːbn̩ viːɐ̯ ˈhɔɪ̯tə] | What day is it today? |
| Heute ist Montag.<br>[ˈhɔɪ̯tə ɪst ˈmoːnˌtaːk] | It's Monday. |
| Welches Datum haben wir heute?<br>[ˈvɛlçɐs ˈdaːtʊm ˈhaːbn̩ viːɐ ˈhɔɪ̯tə] | What date is it today? |
| Es ist der 10. Januar.<br>[ɛs ɪst deːɐ̯ t͡seːn ˈjanuaːɐ̯] | It's the 10th of January. |
| Ist heute ein Feiertag?<br>[ɪst ˈhɔɪ̯tə aɪ̯n ˈfʁaɪ̯taːk] | Is today a holiday? |

1

**Januar**

[ˈjanuaːɐ̯]

January

2

**Februar**

[ˈfeːbʁuaːɐ̯]

February

5

**Mai**

[maɪ̯]

May

6

**Juni**

[ˈjuːni]

June

9

**September**

[zɛpˈtɛmbɐ]

September

10

**Oktober**

[ɔkˈtoːbɐ]

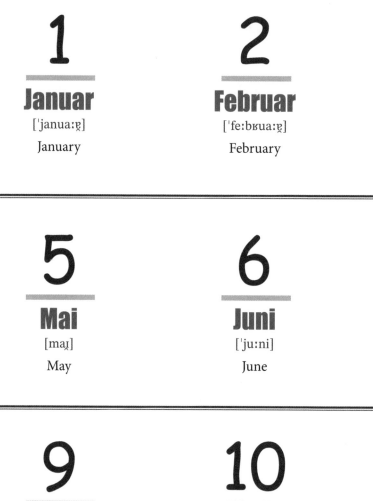

October

## The twelve months of the year

Die zwölf Monate des Jahres [diː t͡svœlf ˈmoːnatə dɛs ˈjaːʁəs]

3

**März**

[mɛʁt͡s]

March

4

**April**

[aˈpʁɪl]

April

7

**Juli**

[ˈjuːli]

July

8

**August**

[aʊ̯ˈgʊst]

August

11

**November**

[noˈvɛmbɐ]

November

12

**Dezember**

[deˈt͡sɛmbɐ]

December

# The weather and seasons

Das Wetter und die Jahreszeiten [das ˈvɛtɐ ʊnt diː ˈjaːʁəsˌt͡saɪ̯tən]

| | |
|---|---|
| der Frühling<br>[deːɐ̯ ˈfʁyːlɪŋ]<br>spring | der Sommer<br>[deːɐ ˈzɔmɐ]<br>summer |
| der Herbst<br>[deːɐ̯ hɛʁpst]<br>autumn | der Winter<br>[deːɐ̯ ˈvɪntɐ]<br>winter |

| | |
|---|---|
| Wie ist das Wetter heute? | What's the weather like today? |
| [viː ɪst das ˈvɛtɐ ˈhɔɪ̯tə] | |
| Das Wetter ist heute schön. | The weather is fine today. |
| [das ˈvɛtɐ ɪst ˈhɔɪ̯tə ʃøːn] | |
| Die Sonne scheint. | It's sunny. |
| [diː ˈzɔnə ʃaɪ̯nt] | |
| Das Wetter ist heute schlecht. | The weather is bad today. |
| [das ˈvɛtɐ ɪst ˈhɔɪ̯tə ʃlɛçt] | |
| Es ist heiß. | It is hot. |
| [ɛs ɪst haɪ̯s] | |
| Es ist sehr heiß. | It is very hot. |
| [ɛs ɪst zeːɐ̯ haɪ̯s] | |
| Mir ist sehr heiß. | I'm boiling. |
| [miːɐ̯ ɪst zeːɐ̯ haɪ̯s] | |
| Es ist sehr kalt. | It's really cold. |
| [ɛs ɪst zeːɐ̯ kalt] | |
| Mir ist sehr kalt. | I'm freezing. |
| [miːɐ̯ ɪst zeːɐ̯ kalt] | |
| Es ist windig. | It's windy. |
| [ɛs ɪst zeːɐ ˈvɪndɪç] | |
| Es ist neblig. | It's foggy. |
| [ɛs ɪst ˈneːblɪç] | |
| Es regnet. | It's rainy. |
| [ɛs ˈʁeːgnət] | |
| Es nieselt. | It's drizzling. |
| [ɛs ˈniːzl̩t] | |
| Es schneit. | It's snowing. |
| [ɛs ˈʃnaɪ̯t] | |

die Stirn
[diː ʃtɪʁn] forehead

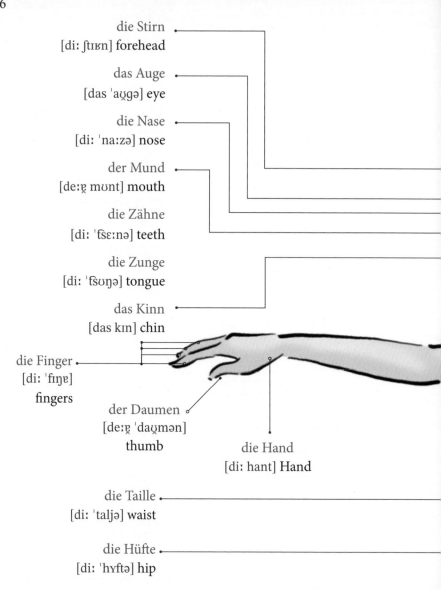

das Auge
[das ˈaʊ̯gə] eye

die Nase
[diː ˈnaːzə] nose

der Mund
[deːɐ̯ mʊnt] mouth

die Zähne
[diː ˈt͡sɛːnə] teeth

die Zunge
[diː ˈt͡sʊŋə] tongue

das Kinn
[das kɪn] chin

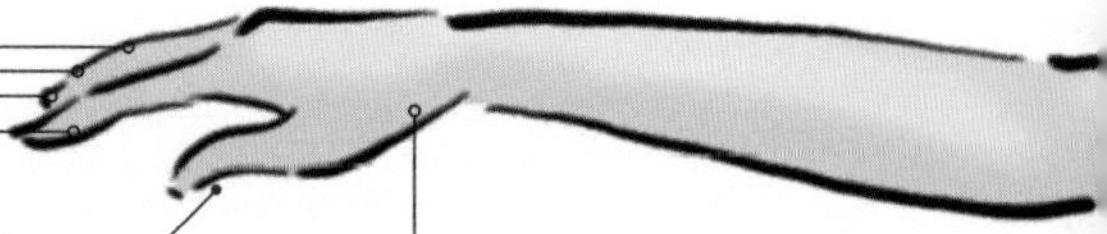

die Finger
[diː ˈfɪŋɐ]
fingers

der Daumen
[deːɐ̯ ˈdaʊ̯mən]
thumb

die Hand
[diː hant] Hand

die Taille
[diː ˈtaljə] waist

die Hüfte
[diː ˈhʏftə] hip

# Parts of the body

Die Körperteile [diː ˈkœʳpɐtael]

der Kopf
[deːɐ̯ kɔpf] head
das Gesicht
[das gəˈzɪçt] face
das Ohr
[das oːɐ̯] ear
die Wange
[diː ˈvaŋə] cheek
der Hals
[deːɐ̯ hals] neck

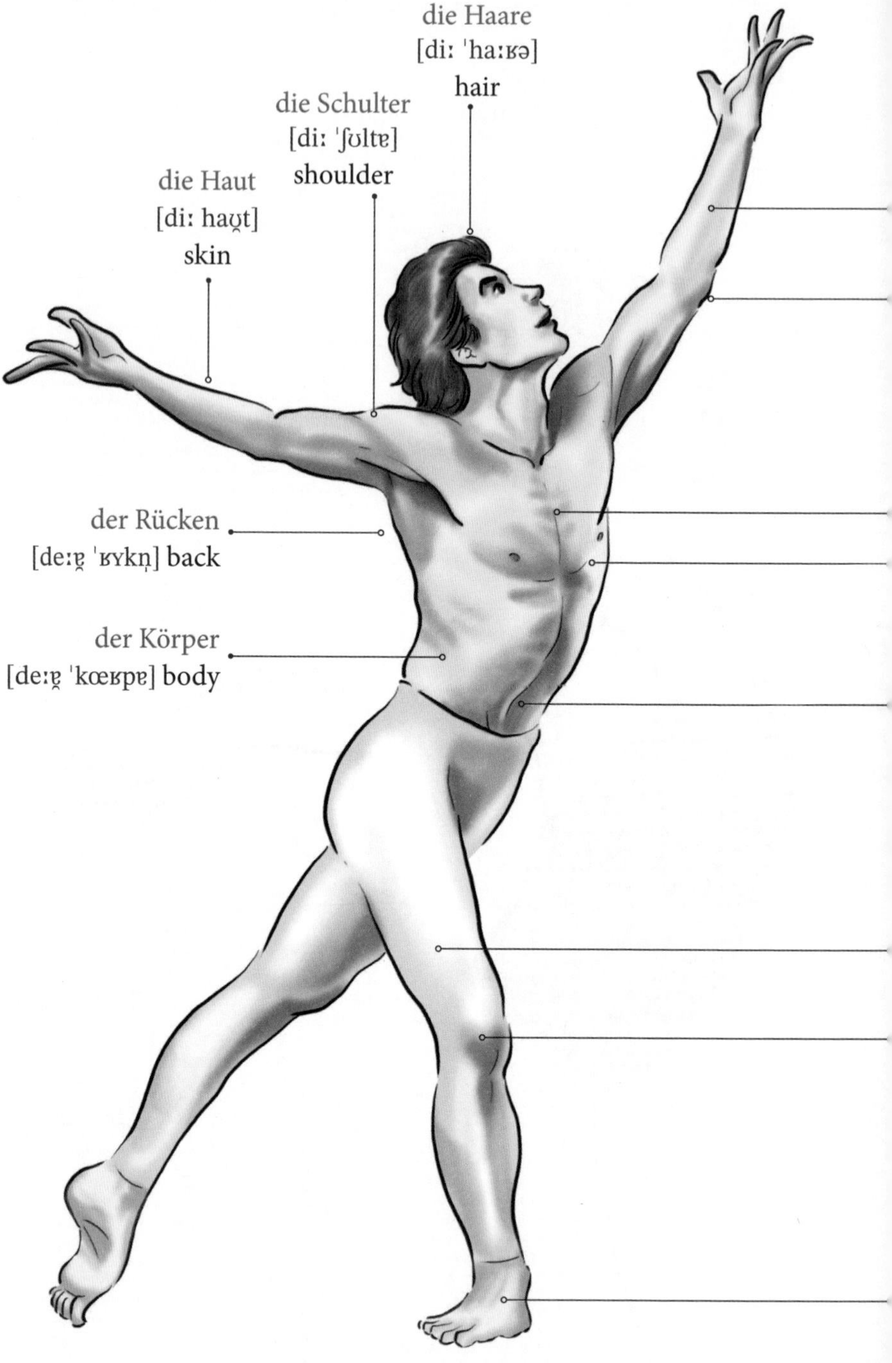
die Haare
[diː ˈhaːʁə]
hair
die Schulter
[diː ˈʃʊltɐ]
shoulder
die Haut
[diː haʊ̯t]
skin
der Rücken
[deːɐ̯ ˈʁʏkn̩] back
der Körper
[deːɐ̯ ˈkœʁpɐ] body

der Arm
[deːɐ̯ aʁm] arm

der Ellbogen
[deːɐ̯ ˈɛlˌboːɡn̩] elbow

die Brust
[diː bʁʊst] chest

das Herz
[das hɛʁt͡s] heart

der Bauch
[deːɐ̯ baʊ̯x] stomach

das Bein
[das baɪ̯n] leg

das Knie
[das kniː] knee

der Fuß
[deːɐ fuːs] foot

# When you feel sick

Wenn man sich krank fühlt [vɛn man zɪç kraŋk fyːlt]

| | |
|---|---|
| Ich bin krank.<br>[ɪç bɪn kʁaŋk] | I don't feel well. |
| Ich muss mich übergeben.<br>[ɪç mʊs mɪç yːbɐˈgeːbn̩] | I need to vomit. |
| Mir ist übel.<br>[miːɐ̯ ɪst ˈyːbl̩] | I feel nauseous. |
| Hier tut es weh.<br>[hiːɐ̯ tuːt ɛs veː] | It hurts here. |
| Ich habe Fieber.<br>[ɪç ˈhaːbə ˈfiːbɐ] | I have a fever. |
| Ich habe Kopfschmerzen.<br>[ɪç ˈhaːbə ˈkɔp͡f‿ʃmɛʁt͡sən] | I have a headache. |
| Ich habe Bauchschmerzen.<br>[ɪç ˈhaːbə ˈbaʊ̯x‿ʃmɛʁt͡sn̩] | I have a stomachache. |

| | |
|---|---|
| Ich habe Halsschmerzen.<br>[ɪç ˈhaːbə ˈhalsˌʃmɛʁt͡sən] | I have a sore throat. |
| Ich habe Rückenschmerzen.<br>[ɪç ˈhaːbə ˈʁʏkn̩ˌʃmɛʁt͡sn̩] | I have a backache. |
| Ich habe Zahnschmerzen.<br>[ɪç ˈhaːbə ˈt͡saːnˌʃmɛʁt͡sn̩] | I have a toothache. |
| Ich habe Verstopfung.<br>[ɪç ˈhaːbə fɛɐ̯ˈʃtɔp͡fʊŋ] | I am constipated. |
| Ich habe Durchfall.<br>[ɪç ˈhaːbə ˈdʊʁçˌfal] | I have a diarrhoea. |
| Ich habe eine Allergie.<br>[ɪç ˈhaːbə ˈaɪ̯nə ˌalɛʁˈgiː] | I have an allergy. |
| Ich habe einen Ausschlag.<br>[ɪç ˈhaːbə ˈaɪ̯nən ˈaʊ̯sʃlaːk] | I have a rash. |

# die Apotheke

[diː apoˈteːkə] pharmacy

## das Krankenhaus

[das ˈkʁaŋkn̩ˌhaʊ̯s] hospital

## die Medizin

[diː mediˈt͡siːn] medicine

## der Arzt / die Ärztin

[deːɐ̯ aːɐ̯t͡st / diː ˈɛːɐ̯t͡stɪn] doctor

## der Zahnarzt / die Zahnärztin

[deːɐ̯ ˈt͡saːnˌʔaːɐ̯t͡st / diː ˈt͡saːnˌʔɛːɐ̯t͡stɪn] dentist

## der Augenarzt / die Augenärztin

[deːɐ̯ ˈaʊ̯gənˌʔaːɐ̯t͡st / diː ˈaʊ̯gənˌʔɛːɐ̯t͡stɪn] optometrist

## der Krankenpfleger / die Krankenschwester

[deːɐ̯ ˈkʁaŋkn̩ˌp͡fleːgɐ / diː ˈkʁaŋkŋ̍ʃvɛstɐ ɐ] nurse

## der Krankenwagen

[deːɐ̯ ˈkʁaŋkn̩ˌvaːgn̩] ambulance

**Gesundheit!**

[gəˈzʊnthai̯t]

Bless you!

Hatschi!

# Urgency

Notfälle [ˈnoːtˌfɛlə]

**Wo ist die Toilette?**

[voː ɪst diː to̯aˈlɛtə]

Where is the toilet?

**Ich muss zur Toilette gehen.**

[ɪç mʊs tsuːɐ̯ to̯aˈlɛtə ˈgeːən]

I need to go to the toilet.

## Gibt es hier eine öffenliche Toilette?

[giːpt̥ ɛs hiːɐ̯ ˈaɪ̯nə ˈœfn̩tlɪç to̯aˈlɛtə]

Is there a public toilet near here?

**Ich muss sofort ins Krankenhaus.**

[ɪç mʊs zoˈfɔʁt ɪns ˈkʁaŋkn̩ˌhaʊ̯s]

I need to go to the hospital.

**Rufen Sie bitte die Polizei!**

[ˈʁuːfn̩ ziː ˈbɪtə diː ˌpoliˈt͡saɪ̯]

Call the police, please!

# What do these signs mean?

Was sagen uns die Schilder? [vas ˈzaːgn̩ ʊns diː ˈʃɪldɐ]

ACHTUNG

ACHTUNG

[ˈaxtʊŋ]

WARNING

Bitte nicht
Stören...

BITTE NICHT STÖREN

[ˈbɪtə nɪçt ˈʃtøːʁən]

DO NOT DISTURB

GESPERRT

[gəˈʃpɛʁt]

RESTRICTED AREA

Hochspannung
Lebensgefahr

HOCHSPANNUNG
LEBENSGEFAHR

[ˈhoːxˌʃpanʊŋ ˈleːbn̩sgəˌfaːɐ̯]

HIGH VOLTAGE
DANGER OF DEATH

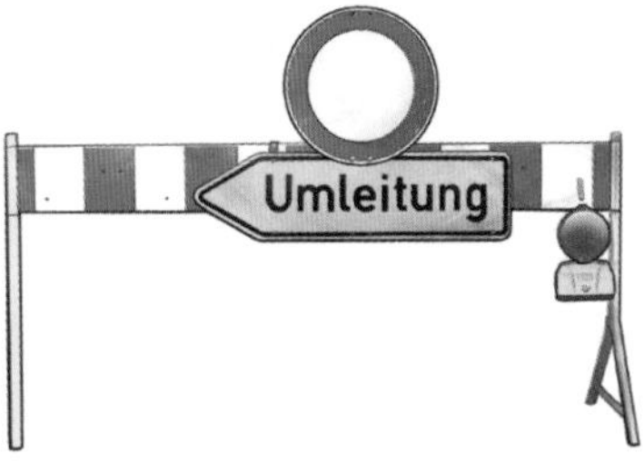
Umleitung

UMLEITUNG

[ˈʊmˌlaɪ̯tʊŋ]

DETOUR

Anlieger
frei

ANLIEGER FREI

[ˈanliːgɐ frae]

OPEN FOR RESIDENTS ONLY

P

PARKPLATZ
[ˈpaʁkˌplat͡s]

PARKING LOT

Einbahnstraße

EINBAHNSTRAßE
[ˈaɪ̯nbaːnˌʃtʁaːsə]

ONE WAY

PARKEN VERBOTEN
[ˈpaʁkn̩ fɛɐ̯ˈboːtn̩]

NO PARKING

Ein- und Ausfahrt
Tag und Nacht
freihalten!
Widerrechtlich abgestellte Fahrzeuge
werden kostenpflichtig abgeschleppt!

EIN-UND AUSFAHRT
TAG UND NACHT FREIHALTEN
[aɪ̯n ʊnt aʊ̯sˈfaːɐ̯t taːk ʊnt naxt ˈfʁaɪ̯ˌhaltn̩]

PUBLIC PARKING PROHIBITED

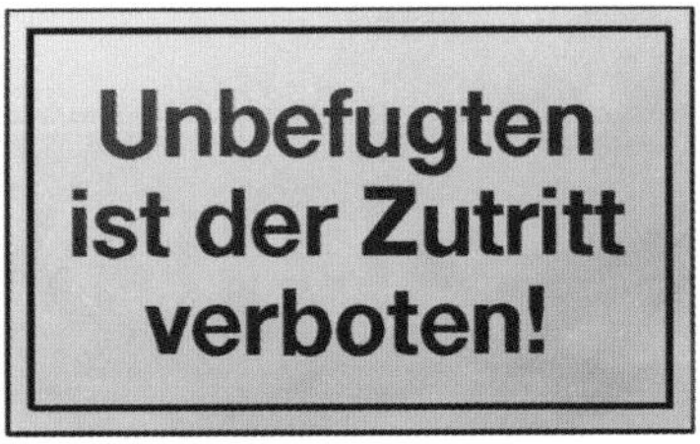
Unbefugten
ist der Zutritt
verboten!

UNBEFUGTEN IST
DER ZUTRITT VERBOTEN
[ˈʊnbəˌfuːktn̩ ɪst deːɐ̯ ˈt͡suːtʁɪt fɛɐ̯ˈboːtn̩]

AUTHORIZED PERSONNEL ONLY

Achtung,
Schule!

ACHTUNG SCHULE
[ˈaxtʊŋ ˈʃuːlə]

CAUTION SCHOOL

ZUTRITT
verboten !
Zutritt nur für Personal.

ZUTRITT NUR FÜR PERSONAL

[ˈt͡suːtʁɪt nuːɐ̯ fyːɐ̯ pɛʁzoˈnaːl]

STAFF ONLY

ZONE

FUSSGÄNGERZONE

[ˈfuːsɡɛŋɐˌt͡soːnə]

PEDESTRIAN ZONE

GEÖFFNET

GEÖFFNET

[ɡəˈʔœfnət]

OPEN

GESCHLOSSEN

GESCHLOSSEN

[ɡəˈʃlɔsn̩]

CLOSED

DRÜCKEN

DRÜCKEN

[ˈdʁʏkn̩]

PUSH

ZIEHEN

ZIEHEN

[ˈt͡siːən]

PULL

Selbst-
bedienung

SELBSTBEDIENUNG
[ˈzɛlpstbəˌdiːnʊŋ]

SELF-SERVICE

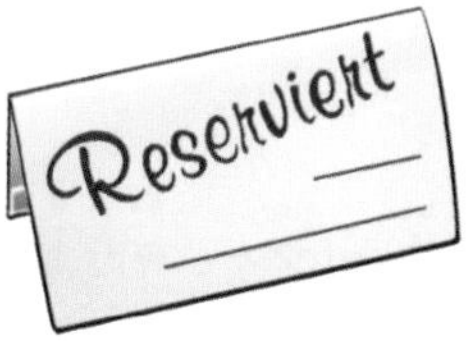
Reserviert

RESERVIERT
[ʁezɛʁˈviːɐ̯t]

RESERVED

DAMEN

DAMENTOILETTE
[ˈdaːməntoa̯ˌlɛtə]

WOMEN

HERREN

HERRENTOILETTE
[ˈhɛʁən toa̯ˌlɛtə]

MEN

FLUCHTWEG
[ˈflʊxtˌveːk]

FIRE EXIT

NOTAUSGANG
[ˈnoːtʔaʊ̯sˌgaŋ]

EMERGENCY EXIT

# Emotional Outbursts

In this chapter we will be dealing with something rather special: emotional outbursts. What, you may ask, does this have to do with a book aimed at introducing a foreign language?

I know that this is quite a sensitive issue, and I'm pretty sure that you don't know any other language books that deal with the topic. As I say, I'm inviting you on a risky adventure. But I think it's absolutely essential for you and really useful. I think you need to know this because it can help you to avoid very embarrassing situations when you are in Germany.

First, let me explain what I mean by emotional outbursts. What exactly are they? They are words that simply tumble out of your mouth. You don't usually give them a second thought – they just pop out – and can't be popped back in again, once they're out

When we are angry, disappointed, afraid, surprised or delighted, we use emotional outbursts to let off steam and regain our calm. We can think of them as turbulence tranquilizers for our emotions.

These outbursts can be more or less violent, depending on intonation and the particular intention or situation in which they are spoken. Gentle outbursts can be mumbled to ourselves to cool our spirits. Violent emotional outbursts are often insulting and deeply hurtful. This type is known in German as Schimpfwörter.

So, you can probably now appreciate how difficult and tricky this whole topic is. These words and phrases are used unconsciously all the time all over the world. The fact that I bring up this topic may be unpleasant for the Germans who are often reserved and polite by nature. However, my intentions are entirely good. I don't want to insult or ridicule their language, but simply to help you avoid making a fool of yourself.

If you hear these German words and try to copy them, it's more than likely that you'll get the exact intonation wrong, or it won't come out at quite the right moment, or be appropriate for the person or situation you're in.

So, my first tip is: don't block your ears when you hear them, but don't just copy them either. As a foreigner, you need to get to know them but use them carefully, and only if you're absolutely certain about how and when.

But even if you never use these outbursts yourself, it is certainly helpful to know them. It might avoid a few embarrassing situations or even a slap in the face. This is one of the main reasons for dealing with these phrases.

I hope I've been able to make clear why this topic is an important one in language learning.

Now let's get started:

The first word we will be looking at is the word "Scheiße!". Don't worry – your own language almost certainly has an equivalent expression. What's more, the literal meaning is really quite banal and describes the organic waste product from our digestive system. That's not really so bad, is it?

Of course, it's not this literal meaning that is intended when this word is used as an emotional outburst. What the expression means in this case is that the present situation or circumstance is as unpleasant and disgusting as direct contact with digestive waste.

Here's a classic example of such a situation: you desperately need to relieve yourself, but the only toilet you find is occupied. You can't hold back much longer and in desperation you shout out "Scheiße!"

For you. With a bit of luck, the current occupant will take note of your desperation and vacate the WC in time.

WC

Another common outburst which is not quite as strong is the word "Mensch!". Once again, this word is not really a swear word. Why have I then included it in this category of emotional outbursts?

The expression is certainly not referring to a specific person. The word is used in much the same way as words such as "Mist!", "Verflixt!" and "Donnerwetter!". All four of these expressions are similar and can be used in similar situations. I can give you a typical example which will help you to understand the meaning.

Imagine the scene: you are preparing a meal for your sweetheart. You don't have much time, and you want everything to be perfect. But fate is not on your side. You try to do everything at once and end up burning the main course. You only have the salad left, and now you have to see what you can do to save the situation.

The outburst "Mensch!", "Mist!", "Verflixt!" or "Donnerwetter!" will give you the opportunity to let off steam and calm down.

The expressions we have looked at so far are used mainly in situations when you are alone. The second group of words are used when you have company. You can shout these expressions at your partner if they have annoyed or disappointed you in any way:

"Idiot!",
"Depp!",
"Doof!",
"Blöde Kuh!"
"Blödmann!"

All these expressions have in common that they indicate that the speaker thinks his (or her) partner are not "quite with it". They clearly suggest that the person in question is stupid, has acted stupidly or incorrectly and needs to be told so in no uncertain terms.

Words like "Idiot!", "Depp!" and "Doof!" are not gender-specific, whereas the term "Blöde Kuh!" clearly refers to a woman, and "Blödmann!" to a man.

The next set of expressions are slightly more controversial. To avoid embarrassing any German who may pick up this book and discover a rude swearword, I will use a kind of code when dealing with the next expressions. This involves avoiding the use of the word itself, and instead using an official spelling alphabet. This will take some of the rudeness out of the expressions. In addition, it has the small side effect of helping you to spell German words.

OK? Now let's go for the more hardcore German outbursts.

The first coded word is spelt: Anton, Richard, Samuel, Cäsar, Heinrich, Ludwig, Otto, Cäsar, Heinrich. This expression compares the person in question to the exit point of our digestive system. This outburst can be used in many differing contexts. However, all these contexts share a significant portion of anger. It definitely indicates that the speaker feels hurt and very likely angry or upset. Unfortunately, it is in very common use.

Here's a classic example of when you might use this word: you happen to meet your ex, who has just left you, escorting two young beauties down the street, or your best friend invites you out to dinner in an expensive restaurant but then turns to you when the waiter brings the bill.

The last German outbursts we will be looking at are the strongest. We all know that certain women follow what we could call a "lying-down" profession. Naturally, some of these women may have sons. If you want to suggest in German that the person you are referring to is such a son, you can call him a Heinrich, Ulrich, Richard, Emil, Nordpol, Samuel, Otto, Heinrich, Nordpol. Of course, we all know that this is not literally true. What we really want to do is to insult and offend the person in question.

Finally, dear readers, let me assure you that I have tried to do all I can to deal with such a sensitive and controversial issue without embarrassing you. I strongly believe that it is important to give you as much confidence as possible when starting to learn the German language.

Knowing something about how people express their feelings and emotions is part of that process. I could continue on this theme for some time, but it's enough for you to have a clear idea of the topic, so that you can avoid any embarrassing situations.

Never forget that emotional outburst can vary in meaning as well as in intensity. They are used by all levels of society, and you'll find them used both by fine old society ladies and socially-deprived youngsters.

If you hear one of these phrases, see if you can hear whether the speaker is angry, dissatisfied, furious, or perhaps cracking a joke or making fun of someone.

As far as possible, avoid using these outbursts yourself. Remember, that these words have the power to insult and hurt others and can also be dangerous for you. By using them, you are likely to put yourself in a very embarrassing situation, and you may quite possibly lose face in the process.

Bravo!

[ˈbʁaːvo]

Bravo!

Genial!

[geˈni̯aːl]

Brilliant!

Super!

[ˈzuːpɐ]

Super!

Einwandfrei!

[ˈai̯nvantˌfʁai̯]

Perfect

# Compliment

Komplimente [ˌkɔmpliˈmɛntə]

Wunderbar!
[ˈvʊndɐbaːɐ̯]
Wonderful!
Herrlich!
[ˈhɛʁlɪç]
Magnificient!

# Romance

Romantisches [ʁoˈmantɪʃəs]

Du bist sehr hübsch.
[duː bɪst zeːɐ̯ hʏpʃ] You are so handsome / beautiful.

Du hast schöne Augen.
[duː hast ˈʃøːnə ˈaʊ̯gn̩] You have got beautiful eyes.

Du bist außergewöhnlich.
[duː ˈbɪst ˈaʊ̯sɐgəˌvøːnlɪç] You are unique.

Ich mag dich sehr.
[ɪç maːk dɪç zeːɐ̯] I like you very much.

Ich liebe dich.
[ɪç ˈliːbə dɪç] I love you.

Ich liebe dich sehr.
[ɪç ˈliːbə dɪç zeːɐ̯] I love you very much.

# Du bist so schön.

[duː ˈbɪst zoː ʃøːn]

You are so beautiful.

# Du bist wundervoll.

[duː ˈbɪst ˈvʊndɐˌfɔl]

You are splendid.

# Ich liebe dich.

[ɪç ˈliːbə dɪç]

I love you.

# Willst du mich heiraten?

[vɪlst duː mɪç ˈhaɪ̯ʁaːtn̩]

Will you marry me?

# Du bist bezaubernd.

[duː ˈbɪst bəˈt͡saʊ̯bɐnt]

You are gorgeous.

# Land and people

Land und Leute [lant ʊnt ˈlɔi̯tə]

DENMARK
NORTH SEA
BALTIC SEA
Kiel
Schleswig-Holstein
Hamburg
Schwerin
Mecklenburg-Vorpommern
POLAND
Bremen
Hamburg
Bremen
Niedersachsen
Berlin
Hannover
Brandenburg
NETHERLANDS
Magdeburg
Nordrhein-Westfalen
Sachsen-Anhalt
Erfurt
Sachsen
Dresden
Düsseldorf
Köln
Thüringen
BELGIUM
Rheinland-Pfalz
Hessen
Wiesbaden
Fankfurt a.M.
CZECH REPUBIC
LUXEMBURG
Saarbrücken
Baden-Württemberg
Bayern
Stuttgart
FRANCE
München
Bodensee
AUSTRIA
SWITZERLAND

If you want to learn about the shape and form of Germany, the simplest thing to do is to look at a map. If you want to know more about the people, how they think, how they lead their lives, then the best method is to look at their proverbs. They reveal how the Germans tick.

Often proverbs have developed over centuries as the result of local people's experiences and of the way they think and live their lives. These sayings are passed on from one generation to the next, together with the emotions and moods they convey. Here are a few memorable German proverbs:

Übung macht den Meister.
[ˈyːbʊŋ maxt deːn maɪ̯stɐ]
Practice makes perfect.

Erst denken, dann handeln.
[ɛʁst ˈdɛŋkn̩ dan ˈhandl̩n]
Think first, then act.

Aus Schaden wird man klug.
[aʊ̯s ˈʃaːdn̩ vɪʁt man kluːk]
One learns from one's mistakes.

Anfangen ist leicht, beharren eine Kunst.
[ˈanˌfaŋən ɪst laɪ̯çt bəˈhaʁən ˈaɪ̯nə kʊnst]
Starting is easy, but preseverance is an art.

Kümmere dich nicht um ungelegte Eier.
[ˈkʏməʁə dɪç nɪçt ʊm ˈʊngəˌleːktə ˈaɪər]
Don't cross your bridges before you come to them.

Now you will be able to savour the German language like a delicatessen. Any worries you may have had about learning this language will turn to joyful confidence.

# German
at your Fingertips

by
**Tien Tammada**

**Original title:** เยอรมันทันใจพูดได้ด้วยปลายนิ้ว

63/120 Moo 8, Tambon Saothonghin, Bangyai District,
Nonthaburi 11140 Thailand
E-Mail: leelaaphasa2008@gmail.com


1. Edition 2023 (1,01 - 2023)


**Translation:** Ta Tammadien, Hubert Möller, David Thorne
**Proofreader:** Kidan Patanant, Klangjai Patanant
**Cover Design:** Sira Illner, Leonie Eul
**Illustrations Interior:** K. Kiattisak, Netitorn Teudbankird
**Photo Credit Cover:** Brandenburg Gate: Shutterstock, KUCO; pretzel: Shuttersock, derGriza; VW Beetle: Shutterstock, Vectorfair
**Typesetting/Layout:** Wachana Leuwattananon, Vipoo Lerttasanawanish
**Printing:** Multiprint GmbH, Konstinbrod

ISBN 978-3-12-514555-9